Daddy
from
Valerie

Extra Nutty!

ALSO BY
Ted L. Nancy

Letters from a Nut
More Letters from a Nut

Extra Nutty!

Even More
Letters
from a Nut

Ted L. Nancy

BACKWORD BY Jerry Seinfeld

St. Martin's Press ✿ New York

ISBN 0-312-26155-1

10 9 8 7 6 5 4

A big thank you to:

Elizabeth Beier (a really nice person), Michael Connor, Susan Boehm, Dr. William Gifford, Dr. Doug Schreck, Dr. Ivan Jonas, Dr. Mickey Weisberg, Dr. Jeana Libed, Dr. M. Robbins, Dr. Vogel, Dr. Curt Olesen, Christopher Lewis, Neil Meyer, Gary Nakashian, Matt Lichtenberg, Bob Ott, Heather Florence, BPM, BB.

Marilyn, John, Justin, Sloppy, Pip The Mighty Squeak, Cookie, Bert, Mark, Donnie, Lou, Stacy, Scott, Hy, Annette, Hallie, Nancy, Michael, Stanley, Lou, Sylvia, Poopsie, Sun Rae, Stacy Peanut, Marty, Dee, Ellen, Jane, Hershel Pearl Judas, Cele, George, Nabar, Sharon, Julie, Justin, Lee, Al, Marge, Linda, Phillip, Dave, Susan, Connie, Ben, Topps the Slender Giant, R.M.A.

Phyllis Murphy should be singled out and saluted! She is one of the greatest human beings I have ever met! (And I have met a lot.)

Dan Strone is indispensable. Impossible to go on without him. A world of a lot of Dan Strones is not so bad. Very nice man.

Jerry Seinfeld—Connected at the soul; like the air in my lungs.

Not Dedicated To:

This book is NOT DEDICATED to those people who DID NOT help me. And you know who you are. I am sick of you.

Once again: I WILL NOT dedicate this book to those people that DID NOTHING for me. You are ZEROS and will not be made mention of here. You know who I'm talking about. I do not like you. You out there know who you are.

T.L.N.

Extra Nutty!

A GOOD FOOL
IS TOUGH TO FIND

But Here I Am

560 No. Moorpark Rd.
#236
Thousand Oaks, CA 91360

Health Permits
Health Department
SALT LAKE CITY
288 N 1460 W
Salt Lake City, UT 84116-3100   Feb 6, 1998

Dear Salt Lake City Health Dept.:

Soon I will be opening "Al Gore's Chinese Restaurant." We are NOT
affiliated with the Vice President in any way. He has nothing to
do with our restaurant. (Although his picture will be in the
window.)   We will have sub gum, moo goo, and spring rolls. So
come on down to "Al Gore's Chinese Restaurant."

We may also carry glum pog, lei mag, and Tums. This is fine
Chinese food with Al Gore's picture in the window. Again, we are
not associated with the current Vice President of the United
States. We are strictly a Chinese restaurant in a mall. Although
we may play Al Gore's speeches through our PA system as diners
enjoy our poo pee, tew ling, and fudge pun.

Please advise on what health permits I need to open my restaurant.
I look forward to hearing from you soon. And please stop in for a
discount squirrel sandwich   (We leave the tail on).

I look forward to hearing from you soon with health permit
information. Thank you. Salt Lake City is a great place!

Sincerely,

Ted L. Nancy
Ted L. Nancy
Mgr, Al Gore's Chinese Restaurant

ENVIRONMENTAL HEALTH DIVISION
1954 East Fort Union Boulevard #100
Salt Lake City, UT 84121
801-944-6608 Fax

Division Director
Terry Sadler
801-944-6600

February 18, 1998

Ted L. Nancy
560 N Moorpark Rd
Thousand Oaks, CA 91360

Dear Mr Nancy,

The letter you sent to the Utah State Health Department has been sent to me for a response. The Salt Lake City/County Health Department, Bureau of Food Protection has jurisdiction over food service facilities in Salt Lake County. Your letter described a restaurant called <u>Al Gore's Chinese Restaurant.</u>

You will need to apply for a business license with the local municipality licensing agent. You did not indicate the address of the facility so I cannot tell you where that is. You also need to submit plans to this office for review, apply for a health department permit and pay the applicable fees and register a manager certified in food safety with us.

I am enclosing paper work to expedite your applications.

Please let us know the address of the restaurant so we may assign an inspector to work with you.

Sincerely,

Daniel A. White, Director
Bureau of Food Protection

560 No. Moorpark Rd. Apt #236
Thousand Oaks, CA 91360   USA

Apr 22, 1999

Information
GERMAN DENTAL ASSOCIATION
Institut der Deutschen Zahnarzte
Universitatsstrabe 71-73
50931 Koln
Postfach 410169
50861 Koln

Dear German Dental Association:

I need help. You have been highly recommended to me by circus
people and a pine cone salesman. I hear you are the most
dedicated dentist facility in the world and that Germany is proud
of you. I have heard of you as far away as Thousand Oaks.
Please help me.

I want to have all my teeth removed and dog teeth put in their
place. I've got 36 Chihuahua teeth that I want exchanged where my
teeth are now. (These are NOT Cinnamon's teeth)   I find this to
be a better look for me. Can I get them rearranged by height?
Will they be even?   I need this for total cleansing; utter
hygiene; complete sanitary precautions. (Unless you can suggest a
better method.) My dentist here just suggests a simple cleaning
for $65.00 but I don't think so. Am I being fooled? Let's get me
in your chair and go to work! Let's do it!)

Also, can you remove stains from the top teeth and put them on the
bottom teeth? (Someone wants to know) I think they are egg
stains.

Tell me when I can make an appointment to see you, and do you take
circus insurance?

Can you give me a list of German dentists that I can contact?
Thank you for getting back to me on this pressing teeth issue.

Sincerely,

Ted L. Nancy

Bundeszahnärztekammer
Arbeitsgemeinschaft der
Deutschen Zahnärztekammern e. V

Hausadresse: Verbandsgeschäftsstelle
                   Universitätsstraße 71-73
                   50931 Köln (Lindenthal)
Postanschrift: Postfach 41 01 68
                   50861 Köln
                   Telefon (02 21) 40 01-0
                   Telefax (02 21) 40 40 35

Mr. Ted L. Nancy
560 No. Moorpark Rd. Apt. ,236

USA – Thousand Oaks, CA.91360

13.08.99
„nancy"

Dear Mr. Nancy,

we acknowledge receipt of your letter of July 1999 referring to your inquiry of April 1999. We are glad to read the reputation of the high quality standard of dental care in Germany and we thank you for your confidence.

However, we know that dental care and dental research is also on a high level in your country and therefore we recommend to you to submit your case to the American Dental Association, att. Mrs. Helen Mck.Cherrett, 211, East Chicago Ave., Chicago Ill. 60611. ADA will probably be prepared and ready to help you. As important and sophisticated dental treatments often not only require regular control examinations but sometimes also corrections it is in general not reasonable to have such treatments done abroad and far away from at home.

Furthermore, the German Dental Association does not have lists or directories of dentists available who offer particular dental care. However, if you insist in having your treatment done in Germany, we recommend to you to contact the teaching hospitals and we enclose the relevant address list.

Now your question concerning insurance programs. In Germany we have two ways of liquidation of dental fees. Approx. 90% of the population is covered by the Legal Health Insurance. The remaining 10% have mostly contracts with private insurance companies and there liquidation is made according th the private scale of dental fees (which also would apply to you).

We hope that this information is of use for you.

With kind regards,
b.o.

ZA M. Krone

560 N. Moorpark Rd.
#236
Thousand Oaks, CA 91360

Nov 19, 1997

Consumer Questions
OSCAR MAYER MEATS
P.O. Box 7188
Madison, Wisconsin   53707

Dear Consumer Questions:

I want to inject ham in me. I understand you sell the
instructions on how I inject ham into me. It is the Oscar Mayer
Ham Injection System booklet, I believe. Please send me the
information. I want to inject ham in me this Friday.

Also, If I bake a ham at 350 degrees for 5 hours, is that too
much?   And, can ham stay in the refrigerator for a month?   I
look forward to an answer on my questions. Thank you. You are
the best at helping consumers with their concerns and problems.
That is why I like your ham. And I WILL continue to purchase your
ham!

Sincerely,

Ted L. Nancy

Oscar Mayer Consumer Center • P.O. Box 7188 • Madison, WI 53707

January 31, 1998

Mr. Ted Nancy
560 N. Moorpark Road
Number 236
Thousand Oaks, CA 91360

Dear Mr. Nancy:

Thank you for contacting Kraft Foods.

Your request for our pamphlet has been received. Unfortunately, this pamphlet is out of print and there are no plans for making it available again.

I'm enclosing some additional information I hope you will enjoy reading.

Thank you again for writing, and please don't hesitate to contact us again with your comments or questions.

Sincerely,

Kim McMiller
Consumer Response Manager

2230259 / 6114271 / BMG

Enclosure
EDUCATION, OSCAR MAYER FRESHNESS DATING
EDUCATION, OSCAR MAYER READ THE LABEL FACT SHEET
RECIPE, OSCAR MAYER RECIPE PACKET

560 No. Moorpark Rd. Apt #236
Thousand Oaks, CA 91360

Jan 21, 1998

Customer Service
RALPH'S SUPERMARKETS
1100 W. Artesia Blvd.
Compton, CA 90220

Dear Ralph's:

I recently bought a sponge from you. When I got home I used my
sponge then went to sleep. I put my sponge on the kitchen sink.
The next morning when I woke up that sponge was in the bedroom
with me? How did it get there?

Another time I was just sitting in the living room reading when I
looked down. I noticed that that sponge was right by my feet.
How did it get there?

I took that sponge and locked it in a room. All night I heard
banging. That sponge wanted to get out! But I wouldn't let it.
I want to talk to somebody there about the possibility that my
sponge is haunted. Who can I talk to?

I am a normal person, no history of paranormalcy, although I once
had a problem with my Clorox moving from my hallway to my family
room. (And there was some knocking from a closed room with that)

I admire Ralph's because they go out of their way to help their
customers. I am a long time shopper at your stores. Now I need
help. Should I send this sponge to you? Or should I just go back
to the store and get a new one and send you the receipt? Thanks
for answering me.

Sincerely,

Ted L. Nancy

Ted L. Nancy

GROCERY COMPANY

GENERAL OFFICES

P.O. BOX 54143 • LOS ANGELES, CALIFORNIA 90054

Telephone (310) 884-9000

February 6, 1998

Mr. Ted L. Nancy
560 N. Moorpark Rd. Apt #236
Thousand Oaks, California 91360

Dear Mr. Nancy,

Thank you for relaying your experience with a recent purchase of a Ralphs Sponge. At Ralphs, we are committed to maintaining a high quality profile in our Ralphs brand products. To help us accomplish this important objective, our company has a staff of technologists who continually monitor the quality of our private label products to reaffirm compliance with established specifications. Despite such efforts, we are sorry to hear that you were less than satisfied with the performance of this product. We have had no reports of similar situations.

We have forwarded your letter on to the supplier of this product asking that they follow up with you regarding your comments. Our Quality Assurance staff will also be notified so that they may follow up with the evaluation of additional product.

We appreciate your comments and apologize for any inconvenience this may have caused. Concerned customers share with us what we are doing right and often point out areas where we can improve as well. We suggest you return the sponge to you local store for refund. We hope you will give us another chance and continue to purchase our many fine quality Ralphs brand products. We value your patronage and look forward to serving your grocery needs for years' to come.

Respectfully yours,

Barbara Ramey

Enclosure

RALPHS • FOOD 4 LESS • BELL MARKETS • CALA FOODS • FALLEY'S • FOODS CO

560 No. Moorpark Rd. Apt #236
Thousand Oaks, CA 91360

Sep 28, 1998

MS. Barbara Ramey
RALPHS SUPERMARKETS
P.O. Box 54143
Los Angeles, CA 90054

Dear MS. Ramey

Thank you very much for answering my letter concerning the haunted
sponge I bought from a Ralphs store. Ralphs has been and always
will be the only store I shop in for my food and sponge needs.

In your letter to me you said that I would be hearing from the
supplier of this sponge. I have not heard from them. And this
sponge is bad.

Can someone from Ralphs come and get this sponge from me? This
sponge is out to get me. I am afraid.

After I got your letter I went down to my basement and locked that
sponge in a steel box and put a chain around that box. Then I
wrapped that box in tape and put a shackle around that. Then I
boarded up the basement door with over 1000 nails. Then I put a
manacle on that door. Then I went upstairs to my room to get a
good nights sleep.

At about 3 o'clock in the morning I woke up and looked down. That
sponge was right by my bed. I am scared. Please help me.

Also, do you sell Brillo at your store?

When will I hear from the supplier? I need to know. Thank you
for your reply.

Sincerely,

Ted L. Nancy

Ted L. Nancy

Ralphs

GROCERY COMPANY
GENERAL OFFICES
P O BOX 54143
LOS ANGELES CALIFORNIA 90054
Customer Relations

Mr. Ted L. Nancy
560 N. Moorpark Rd. Apt #236
Thousand Oaks, California 91360

560 No. Moorpark Rd.
Suite #236
Thousand Oaks, CA 91360

Sep 15, 1999

Owner
NORMS BARBERSHOP
CAN'T DIVULGE
CAN'T SAY, NV 89---

Dear Norms Barber Shop:

I want to open Gnorms Barber Shop. It will be close to your Norms
Barber Shop.

I am the previous owner of the GNOME SHOP. We sold gnome
figurines. I closed the shop. Now is the time for Gnorms.
Please let me know if you think my barber shop name will be too
confusing. I am a good neighbor and just want to blend in. (May
sell gnome figures at register)

Thank you. I can change my name to something else if you think it
will not be good for you. I am a good gneighbor at Gnorms!
I look forward to hearing from you soon.

Once again, I hope this will gnot be confusing. If it is just
tell me so I can cancel the sign. Thank you.

Sincerely,

Ted L. Nancy
Ted L. Nancy

NORM'S BARBER SHOP
"WE'RE A CUT ABOVE"

September 29, 1999

Mr. Ted L. Nancy
560 No. Moorpark Rd., Suite #236
Thousand Oaks, CA 91360

Dear Mr. Ted L. Nancy:

Sincerely,

Norman Murginn
Owner Norm's Barber Shop

CERTAIN PEOPLE PREVENT ME FROM SHOWING THIS!

560 No. Moorpark Rd.
Suite #236
Thousand Oaks, CA 91360

Oct 6, 1999

MR. NORMAN MURGINN
NORMS BARBERSHOP
CONFIDENTIAL
DELETE, NV 89

Dear Mr. Murginn,

Thank you very much for getting back to me on the similarity of
our name situation. (Re: Your letter of Sep 29, 1999) I
sincerely appreciate it.

After much consideration I have decided not to call my barber shop
Gnorms. You were right that it is too close to your Norms
Barbershop. The public will be confused! So instead, I have
decided to call myself Morms. This should not even be close to
your Norms. But if it is I will try another name. Just let me
know. I want to be a good neighbor.

I will call myself Morms Barbershop. Lets keep the line of
communication open as I plan to open soon my business on CONFIDENTIAL
Street in TOP SECRET, Nevada. (Near You)

I don't think there will be any confusion when I answer the phone
"Morms Barber Shop."

You were right the Gnome shop is too similar. The name is not
good. (Can't hear the G when answering the phone) Once again I
have another name I'm thinking of if Morms is too similar. It's
up to you. Just let me know. I want to do right for the
community Thank you and I look forward to hearing from you.

Soon to be your neighbor,

Ted L. Nancy
Ted L. Nancy
Morms Barber Shop

NORM'S BARBER SHOP
"WE'RE A CUT ABOVE"

October 25, 1999

Mr. Ted L. Nancy
560 No. Moorpark Rd., Suite #236
Thousand Oaks, CA 91360

Dear Mr. Ted L. Nancy:

bad

Sincerely,

Norman Murginn
Norm's Barber Shop

CAN NOT SHOW!

GMORMS BARBER SHOP

G'Morning Gmorms

560 No. Moorpark Rd. Suite #236
Thousand Oaks, CA 91360

Mr. Norman Murginn
WON'T SAY st.
CAN'T TELL, NV 89---   Nov 3, 1999

Dear Mr. Murginn,

Thank you very much for your prompt reply of Oct 25. It was very
nice to hear from you. Yes, you are right Morms - Norm's - it's
too similar. I said it out loud like you said. They DO sound
like Ned and Ted. It is a bad idea.

What about if I call my shop GMORMS? Then there is not so much
similarity. If I answer the phone G'morning Gmorms then you can
hear the new name. And it has a nice ring to it - "G'Morning
Gmorms." I put my logo on top of my stationary (like you have) so
you could see it. If I just answer "Morms barber shop" it is
tough, I have to admit. But now you have to pronounce the G when
you say Good Morning (G'morning) GaMorms.

Yes, I AM a good neighbor. And I WILL make sure you are totally
satisfied with the name before I start my business. My large
bright, flashing sign will not look like Norm's Barber Shop at
all. It will say Gmorms Barber Shop. The first 2 letters are
completely different, so by the time you get to "orms" you're
already off in a new direction.

I am anxious to hear what you feel about this name. Mr. Murginn,
if you really feel it is too similar I will of course, not use it.
Perhaps you can help with a name that you find is satisfactory to
both of us. This can be worked out. We are close. (I don't
like Nroms if you are thinking of that). I will still hand out
Gnomes at the register. Our motto: "Everybody gets a free gnome
at Gmorms (or whatever we call it)." Maybe we could even style
each other's hair some day. I would like that.

Respectfully,

Ted L. Nancy
Gmorms Barber Shop
"Look Neat In The Heat"

NORM'S BARBER SHOP
"WE'RE A CUT ABOVE"

November 15, 1999

Mr. Ted L. Nancy
560 No. Moorpark Rd., Suite #236
Thousand Oaks, CA 91360

Dear Mr. Nancy:

FED UP!

!!

!!

!!

Sincerely,

Norman Murginn
Norm's Barber Shop

SMRON BARBER SHOP

("NORMS BACKWARDS")

560 No. Moorpark Rd. Suite #236
Thousand Oaks, CA 91360

Mr. Norman Murginn
NORMS BARBER SHOP
CLASSIFIED
?, NV 89---   Nov 29, 1999

Dear Mr. Murginn,

First of all, please calm down. You don't have to take that
attitude. I AM a good neighbor. And I sincerely appreciate that
you are trying to work this out with me. And we will work it
out!!! My big flashing sign will not go up until you approve the
name. That is my credence to you. I want to be the best neighbor
on CLASSIFIED Street that I can be!

I was now thinking my name should be: SMRON BARBER SHOP. This is
Norms backwards. Now we have something that is completely
different. Only ambulances and people pulling away from the
barber shop will be able to see the name "Norms" when they look in
their rear view mirror. (And I don't want their business.) I
feel this is completely the reverse of your name. Smron Barber
Shop and Norms Barber Shop next to each other is not confusing.
However, if you feel it is and you don't like it just tell me and
I will continue to try and make you happy. I want to make you
happy, Norm. That is my goal.

I will still hand out gnomes at the register. Our motto: "Grab A
Gnome At Smron." Please let me know if I have made any progress.
I look forward to hearing from you soon as the sign is just
waiting to go up. Thank you and remember - we are good neighbors
to each other. Let's style each other's heads. I'm a cut above
too.

Sincerely,

Ted L. Nancy
Ted L. Nancy
Smron Barber Shop

NORM'S BARBER SHOP
"WE'RE A CUT ABOVE"

December 7, 1999

Mr. Ted L. Nancy
560 No. Moorpark Rd., Suite #236
Thousand Oaks, CA 91360

Dear Mr. Nancy:

cut above

NOT

PLEASE!!!

Sincerely,

Norman Murginn
Norm's Barber Shop

WISH I COULD SHOW – BUT I CAN 'T

MURGINN'S GNOMES

(Formerly Smron Barbershop)

560 N. Moorpark Rd. #236
Thousand Oaks, CA 91360

Mr. Norman Murginn
NORM'S BARBERSHOP
CONCEALED st.
WON'T TELL, NV 89

Dec 15, 1999

Dear Mr. Murginn,

Look, there's no reason to get angry. Who is ruining your life? I am not ruining your life. I have said all the names out loud like you said. Norms, Morms, Gamorms, Smron. They sound alike. So? Anyway, I am happy to tell you that I have decided NOT to open up a barbershop. Instead, I will go back to selling Gnomes.

I would like to call my business Murginn's Gnomes. (If it is OK with you) I like that name a lot. What do you think? Please let me know if you think my gnome gname will be too confusing to your barbershop name. I am a good gneighbor and just want to blend in. (I may sell barber combs at the register) I am opening in WON'T TELL soon and want to get my sign. If you prefer I will NOT call myself Murginn's Gnomes. I can come up with another name but I do like this one. We will soon be gneighbors and I want to get off on the right foot.

I am leaving the * hair cutting to you. I have heard you give the best haircuts in town and would like to get my hair cut by you. Perhaps I can sell you a gnome. They'll have the Murginn name on them. I thought of calling my place Smron Gnomes. But then I thought if I advertised "Free Gnome at Smron" Or "Grab A Gnome At Smron" that it just did not sound right. I MAY hand out smron at the door. I look forward to hearing from you. I hope this will gnot be confusing. My sign is almost ready.

Respectfully,

Ted L. Nancy
Murginn's Gnomes

NORM'S BARBER SHOP
"WE'RE A CUT ABOVE"

January 7, 2000

Mr. Ted L. Nancy
560 No. Moorpark Rd., Suite #236
Thousand Oaks, CA 91360

Dear Mr. Nancy:

           Pinscher!

Sincerely,

Norman Murginn

GMURGINN'S GNOMES

"G'Morning GMurginns"

560 N. Moorpark Rd. #236
Thousand Oaks, CA 91360

Mr. Norm Murginn
NORMS BARBERSHOP
POSITIVELY WILL NOT SAY St.
VEILED, NV 89---   Jan 12, 2000

Dear Mr. Murginn,

I am truly sorry to exasperate you. I really am. That is not my
intention. And no, I am not afraid of a dog. (I am the owner of
Cinnamon) Anyway, I have decided NOT to call myself Murginn's
Gnomes. You were right. The names are similar and too confusing!
And yes, I believe the mail and the parking would be a mess.
Instead, I will call myself G'MURGINNS GNOMES. Then there is not
so much similarity. And this makes it easier when I answer the
phone "G'morning GMurginns Gnomes." I will still hand out barber
combs at the register.

Finally My sign is being prepared now. My sign is LARGE and may
BLOCK the view of some of your name. If I can buy space on your
wall (I know your business is inside a hair salon) I would
appreciate it as I may need to cover part of your Norms Name with
my big flashing sign. I may have to put my sign right in the
middle of your big S.

I look forward to being your gneighbor, you with Norm's Barbershop
and me with GMurginn's Gnomes next to each other. You cutting
hair and me selling gnomes. I am a good neighbor and want to
please you, Mr. Murginn. I hope this solves our problem.

Sincerely,

Ted L. Nancy
G'Murginns!

560 No Moorpark Rd. #236
Thousand Oaks, CA 91360

Jan 26, 2000

Mr. Norman Murginn
NORMS BARBERSHOP
REALLY SECRET st.
OFF THE RECORD, NV, 89

Dear Mr. Murginn,

Norm? Norm, I haven't heard from you in a while. Are you OK? I
wrote to you and have not heard back. I am worried. This is
about the similarity of our names.

Anyway, Good News. I'm NOT using the name Gmurginns Gnomes. I
just don't like it. Gmurginn is a weird name and many people at
the sign company have mispronounced it. They call it JuhMirginn
or Gam-erginn. Anyway, I have a new name. It all of a sudden hit
me. Where have I been?

I will now call my business GNANCY'S GNOMES. Finally an
intellegant answer to my problem. Then I don't need to get your
permission. Thank you for your time. I hope I haven't bothered
you. I hope I haven't disturbed anything. Now I can answer the
phone "Gnight Gnancy's Gnomes." Do you like it? I will see you
on REALLY SECRET Street soon, Norm. (I don't want to confuse our
customers) Thinking of you. Bye.

I have been having dog dreams.

Your Friend,

Ted L. Nancy

Ted L. Nancy
Gnancy's Gnomes
"I'm A Cut Above"

560 No. Moorpark Rd. #236
Thousand Oaks, CA 91360

Feb 22, 1998

Vending Licensing Dept.
Administration Office
CITY OF KING OF PRUSSIA
175 W Valley Forge Rd.
King Of Prussia, PA 19406-1802

Dear Vending License Dept.:

I want to set up my UNDERWEAR VENDING MACHINES in your city.
There are 2,300 of them on corners, near banks, by parks, at
schools. A fella can choose a pair of fresh underwear from a Ted
Nancy portable underwear vending machine and change right there!
(A person should be able to change their underwear in less than 15
seconds. People can't see if the time is kept to).

I also need a permit for my PHONY DOG DOO VENDING MACHINES. I
want to set up 10,100 of them in your city. That's 12,400 vending
machines of underwear and dog doo. One on every block. And maybe
a drive up if you are NOT wearing any shorts.

Your city needs this service. It's about time that a person can
get fresh skivvies and gag crap without having to go to a mall.
Please let me know what permits I need? Thank you.

Also, please let me know if I need a permit to sell corn dogs on
the lawn in front of City Hall? Thank you. I look forward to
hearing from you soon.

Sincerely,

Ted L. Nancy
Vend-A-Fun

UPPER MERION TOWNSHIP
BOARD OF SUPERVISORS

175 WEST VALLEY FORGE ROAD
KING OF PRUSSIA, PA 19406-1802
(610) 265-2600
TELECOPIER: (610) 265-0482

BOARD OF SUPERVISORS

ROBERT G. CLIFTON
CHAIRMAN

BARBARA S. FRAILEY
VICE-CHAIRMAN

RALPH P. VOLPE
ANTHONY J. VOLPI
J. TED LOWE

*TOWNSHIP MANAGER/
SECRETARY-TREASURER*
RONALD G. WAGENMANN

TOWNSHIP SOLICITOR
ALAN E. BOROFF

February 26, 1998

Ted L. Nancy
Vend-A-Fun
560 No. Moorpark Rd.
236
Thousand Oaks, CA 91360

Re: Your letter dated February 22, 1998

Dear Mr. Nancy,

This letter is in response to your inquiry concerning the licensing of vending machines and peddling of food in Upper Merion Township.

Concerning your proposal to install and maintain vending machines for underwear and phony dog doo, Upper Merion Township does permit the installation of vending machines on properly zoned private property with an owners permission, with the owner of the vending machines being required to conform with Chapter 149, titled " Taxation", of the Upper Merion Township Code (a copy of which I have enclosed). However, you would not be permitted to display these machines on any public right-of –way, on any private property without an owners permission or on any property that is not properly zoned to allow the sale of variety merchandise.

Concerning your proposal to sell corn dogs, Upper Merion Township does permit peddling, so long as the activity is done in compliance with Chapter 119, titled "Peddling, Soliciting and Hawking", of the Upper Merion Township Code (a copy of which I have enclosed). The selling of food products would also require you to obtain licenses from the Pennsylvania Department of Environmental Protection and the Montgomery County Health Department. However, your proposal to sell these products on Upper Merion Township property would not be permitted by the Township.

I trust this answers any questions you have, should you require further information, please call me at 610-265-2606 – extension 115.

Sincerely,

John W. Mateja, Jr.
Zoning Officer

JWM:jwm

CC: RGW
FAM
JRW
ML

What people do for themselves dies with them; what people do for their community lives on . .

560 No. Moorpark Rd. Apt #236
Thousand Oaks, Calif. 91360 USA
May 7, 1998

ARGENTINE GOVERNMENT TOURIST OFFICE
5055 Wilshire Blvd.
Suite 210
Los Angeles, CA 90036

Dear Argentina Tourist Office,

Usually people have complaints about a department store. This letter is to PRAISE your fine employees at Glorms Store in Argentina.

On a recent visit, I became stuck in the toilet. It was very embarrassing for all. My entire body was stuck in the commode. Arms, legs, torso, head – everything was in there. This team of people that work at one of your country's finest stores lifted me up and out. I was so embarrassed, but they did they job. I can't believe I fell in the potty. Your entire country should be singled out and commended for service that was far beyond putting pins in shirts.

This is a fine example of why Glorms is a great place to shop at. I will tell everyone I ever meet that Argentina is and Glorms are the finest.

Please write me and let me know you got this letter. And that they were thanked. It is very important to me. Thanks. I love their plus size husky man's chubby stout clothes and rattlesnake socks. I look forward to hearing from you soon.

Also, what time is it in Argentina when it is 2 o'clock in the morning in Phoenix? Thank you.

Sincerely,

Ted L. Nancy

Ted L. Nancy

Argentina
The Land of the Six Continents

Ted L. Nancy   May 15, 1998
560 N. Moorpark Rd. # 236
Thousand Oaks, Ca 91360

Dear Mr. Nancy,

    I have recieved your letter, Thank You! Iám really glad you were satisfied with our service. I did inform the employees that you thank them very much for what they did for you, they said you are very welcome!!!!

    In United States, when the time is 2 p.m. in Argentina it is 7 p.m.. If you have any questions please give me a call, Thank You very much!!!!

Sincerly,

Agustina Cuebras

LET'S GET SLOPPY!

OH YEAH!

560 No. Moorpark Rd.
Suite #236
Thousand Oaks, CA 91360

OCEAN & DOG LICENSING DEPT.
1424 9th Ave.
Helena, MT 59601   Apr 29, 1999

Dear Helena Ocean & Dog Licensing Dept.

Please direct me for my license.

I will stage the play "MARK TWAIN WITH TOURETTES SYNDROME".
This is a vivid reenactment of the great humorist if he had the
barking obscenities disease.

In the performance, Mark Twain will reminisce about Huck Firn on
the Mississippi then yell out a slew of dirty words. Then he will
talk fondly about the old steamer comin' down the river and how it
chugged along then bark out filthy obscenities then back again
talkin about the steamer. The same with the jumping frog. How it
entered a contest in Calavasas and won. Here is a sample from the
play:

The old frog was really jumping that day - Da&mN fu$@in sob piece
of sh*$it frog. It really jumped - that pr&^c#@k fu$)k frog!!"

Language unsuitable to print.

"Mark Twain With Tourettes Syndrome" is a family play (except for
the cursing) suitable for all ages (except for the filth) and kids
and grandmas will especially like the steamboat and frog
reminisces. (If they can get by the harsh "sailor" talk)

Let me know what arrangements I need to make to store my anchovie
tank at your seaport. Thank you. I await large crowds.

Sincerely,

Ted L. Nancy
Ted L. Nancy

Economic
DEVELOPMENT
Montana Department of Commerce

May 3, 1999

Ted L. Nancy
560 N. Moorpark Rd
Suite 236
Thousand Oaks CA 91360

Dear Mr. Nancy:

I received your letter of April 29, 1999. Today I tried calling "information" for a telephone number for you, but your name is not listed. I would appreciate a call from you so that we can discuss your letter. My phone number is 406-444-0449. If I am unavailable when you call, please leave me your name and a day time phone number. I will return your call as soon as possible.

Your request for licensing requirements is rather unusual. What city in Montana do you plan to stage the play about a Tourettes Syndrome re-enactment.

If you plan to stage your play in a city park, please check with each city clerk or parks department for licensing requirements and regulations. The State of Montana does not have an Ocean and Dog Licensing Department.

M.A. Gregory
M.A. Gregory
Program Assistant

560 No. Moorpark Rd. #236
Thousand Oaks, CA 91360

M.A. Gregory
ECONOMIC DEVELOPMENT
1424 9th Ave. POB 200505
Helena, MT 59620-0505   May 17, 1999

Dear M.A. Gregory,

Thank you for writing me back regarding my one man show - "MARK
TWAIN WITH TOURETTES SYNDROME." To answer your questions: The
play is 45 minutes long of which 32 minutes is solid cursing.
Naturally, with Tourettes Syndrome there are large blocks of foul
language. It can get pretty vulgar out there at times. But the
play itself is a lighthearted warm telling of the story of Huck
Finn and Tom Sawyer and their youth in Missouri mingled with
Tourettes vulgarities.

Here is another sample of the show: "Huck and Tom were painting
the fence that day in the hot Missouri sun. Pr*^k! It sure was a
scorcher that day. Mo5&er fu@)k9r. Whew, it was warm. Sh#t!
Co$k B2s&%rd! The frog really jumped far that day to win the
contest. D#ck! It was grand fun indeed. Co<$su#@i]g As)*9le.
As the Steamer came down the Mississippi.

Also, instead of an anchovie tank I may now need a tentful of
pelicans. What is the licensing requirements for that? Pelicans
do smell when in a crowd. (There will be NO pelican barking) My
play will be in Helena, Montana. Will you scrape my shoe? I
sincerely look forward to hearing from you soon as I want to stage
my play in the downtown Civic Center area. The crowds will be
big. Thank you very much. ·

Respectfully,

Ted L. Nancy

Economic DEVELOPMENT
Montana Department of Commerce

1424 9th Avenue • PO Box 200505
Helena, MT 59620-0505

TED NANCY
560 N MOORPARK RD
SUITE 236
THOUSAND OAKS CA 91360

91360-3760 08

560 North Moorpark Road
Suite #236
Thousand Oaks, California
91360

Reservations
MATSUHISA RESTAURANT
129 N. La Cienega Blvd.
Beverly Hills, CA 90211   12/6/96

Dear Reservations,

Soon I will be in the Beverly Hills area to stay for two years. I
must live there because of my physical problems. I want to have
my celebration party at your restaurant.

I want to make a reservation to dine at your magnificent
restaurant on Jan 7, 1996. I have heard it is unparalleled. The
wine cellar is stupendous, the view is breathtaking. I have heard
your food is exceptional. (I like buttery squid).

Because of my medical condition, I must eat with my ear. I feed
myself. Food is deposited into my ear and I eat this way. I can
eat most everything. (No sticky mashed potatoes, please).

Will it be okay to dine in your restaurant on the evening of
Jan 7, 1996? I have heard of your glorious treasures, that your
surroundings are majestic, that your appetizers are scrumptious.

Will eating through my ear be a problem? After a while, people
don't look. If they do, however, I am still pleasant. Let me
know as I am anxious to dine with you. Thank you. I look forward
to hearing from you so I can arrange my celebratory party. This
will be a large party that I want to arrange. Who do I contact?

Respectfully,

Ted L. Nancy

Matsuhisa
Japanese Gourmet Seafood • Sushi

December 20, 1996

To: Mr. Ted L. Nancy
560 North Moorpark Road, Suite 236
Thousand Orks, Ca 91360

From: Eriko Sakai
Matsuhisa Restaurant

Dear Mr. Nancy:

I am sorry to write you back so late.
I just received your letter yesterday from restaurant. I love to have you and your guests on January 7th 1997. Since our restaurant is already over booked that day, I will try to seat you and your party at our private room. But if more than 18 people in your party, unfurtunetry I can't take your reservation.

Could you please call me for time and number of your party as soon as you can? So I can take care of your party. My number is: 310 289-2108, Address: 8671 Wilshire Blvd., #601 Beverly Hills, Ca 90211.

Wish your happy holidays.

Sincerely,

Eriko Sakai
Matsuhisa Restaurant

560 N. Moorpark Rd. #236
Thousand Oaks, CA 91360

Jan 3, 2000

Broker Dept.
CENTURY 21 REALTY
350 E Belle Rd #J205
Phoenix, AZ 85022

Dear Century 21 Realty,

I am seeking your help in finding me retail space for my
store: Really Wet Toothpicks.

Please tell me who I contact in your office to help me in seeking
store space in Phoenix, Arizona. Thank you.

Sincerely,

Ted L. Nancy

Centre Point
350 East Bell Rd, Suite J205
Phoenix, Arizona 85022
(602) 861-3434

Donald L. Kraus
Broker

January 21, 2000

Mr. Ted Nancy
560 N. Moorpark Rd. #236
Thousand Oaks, CA   91360

Dear Mr. Nancy,

Please contact me directly so that we can discuss your Real Estate
needs in the Phoenix area. Our 800 # is 800-487-3405!

Best Regards.

Ron Metzger

Each Office Is Independently Owned And Operated

560 No Moorpark Rd. #236
Thousand Oaks, CA 91360

Feb 1, 2000

Mr. Ron Metzger
CENTURY 21 REALTY
350 E Belle Rd. # J205
Phoenix, AZ 85022

Dear Mr. Metzger,

Thank you for trying to help me find store space for my business:
Really Wet Toothpicks.

You asked for information on my store to help you in selecting the
right space for me. (My real estate needs)

While many say that wet toothpicks are useless because they will
shred in your teeth. I say the buyers are out there. These
toothpicks are easy to fold. Plus, they won't jab you when
they're in your pocket!

Please help me find a suitable store for a long lease, or possibly
a building to buy for many of my stores.

I await your reply with how we proceed on Really Wet Toothpicks.
Thank you.

Sincerely,

Ted L. Nancy

Ted L. Nancy

Ted L. Narey

Ted L. Narey

Sincerely,
    Ted L. Narey

Respectfully,
    Ted L. Narey

Best Regards,
    Ted L. Narey

Ted L. Narey

Ted L. Nancy

Cordially,
Mr. Ted L. Narey

I Remain...
    Ted L. Narey

560 N. Moorpark Rd. #236
Thousand Oaks, CA 91360

Jan 5, 2000

Broker Dept.
COLDWELL BANKER REALTY
1234 S Power Rd. #250
Mesa, AZ 85206

Dear Coldwell Banker Realty,

I am seeking your help in finding me retail space for my
store: Really Dry Glue.

Please tell me who I contact in your office to help me in seeking
store space in Mesa, Arizona. Thank you.

Sincerely,

Ted L. Nancy

SUCCESS REALTY

SUPERSTITION SPRINGS CORP. PLAZA
1234 S POWER RD. #250
MESA, AZ 85206
BUS. (480) 396-7550
FAX (480) 396-7575

Ted L. Nancy
560 N. Moorpark rd. #236
Thousand Oaks, CA   91360

Re: Finding retail space for store: Really Dry glue.

Dear Mr. Nancy:

We have your inquiry letter of 1/5/00.

Other than by postal mail, how do you wish for us to make contact with you.
We need your phone numbers, fax, E-Mail or some quicker way to work with
you. Your letter has no phone number(s).

Also, can you give us more details/criteria.

Arthur Dunbar, Associate Broker

560 No. Moorpark Rd.
Apt #236
Thousand Oaks, CA 91360 USA

Nov 18, 1996

Customer Service
HARRODS DEPARTMENT STORE
87 Brompton Rd., SW1
London, England

Dear Customer Service,

I want to buy your "Hungry Midget Frozen Knuckles." (Mall size, please). I don't see them in the supermarket freezer. Where are they? Also, do you still make the "Hungry Midget Freeze Fried Frozen Frog Fritter Flap Franks?" I haven't seen them in over 12 years. Although I have only looked one place. What about Frozen double toes? These are two toes that are together to form one toe, frozen.

Please send me info on all your frozen 'Midget' foods. they are good. They fit into the lunch box perfectly leaving plenty of room for ointment.

If you do not still stock these perhaps you can suggest gifts that I may purchase from your excellent store. I have heard wonderful things of Harrods Department Store. I have heard you are the premier store for specialty items in London and Cerritos. Wonderful! Thank you. I look forward to hearing from you soon so I can start ordering.

Respectfully,

Ted L. Nancy

KNIGHTSBRIDGE

HARRODS LIMITED, KNIGHTSBRIDGE, LONDON SW1X 7XL. TELEPHONE 0171-730 1234 • TELEX 24319 • FAX 0171-581 0470 • REGISTERED IN LONDON NO 30209
TELEGRAPHIC ADDRESS - EVERYTHING LONDON SW1

28 November 1996

Mr Ted L Nancy
560 No. Moorpark road
Apt #236
Thousand Oaks
CA 91360
USA

Dear Mr Nancy

Thank you for your most interesting letter dated 18 November 1996, which has been passed for my attention from our Customer Services department.

Unfortunately we do not stock, nor to my recollection have we ever stocked any "Hungry Midget" product. However I would be most interested as to what kind of food item are "Hungry Midget Freeze Fried Frozen Frog Fritter Flap Franks".

I trust this is satisfactory, and if you should have any further queries please do not hesitate to contact me.

Yours sincerely

Martyn Wick
Trainee Buyer
Fromagerie and Frosted Foods

560 No. Moorpark Road
Apt #236
Thousand Oaks, CA 91360 USA

Mar 18, 1997

Customer Service Dept.
GENERAL TRADING COMPANY GIFT SHOPPE
144 Sloane St., SW1
London, England

Dear General Trading Company Gift Shoppe,

I am interested in your "FAMISHED DWARF FROZEN DINNERS" which
consist of 9 wings, 2 thighs and a toe in a 6 ounce jar for
children under the age of 6 months. I can't find them in stores
although I have seen them in Kensington. But when will I get back
to Kensington again? (Too many papers to fill out regarding
boils).

I was told that the General Trading Company Gift Shoppe has this
food. Also, do you have frozen baby food? Can I order directly
from you? Please write me with all your baby food line:
Including baby pot roast, baby duck L'orange, and your frozen baby
spinach splatter. Thank you.

I look forward to hearing from you with my request soon. Famished
Dwarf is the finest baby food out there. I have told others this.
Let's all have a good meal!

I wrote to you before but have never heard back. Please
communicate with me. I have heard wonderful things of General
Trading Company. I have heard Princess Diana registered with you
for her wedding. (I sent a poncho from Zodys. I didn't know!) I
would like to buy many things from you. Is there a special
salesperson I should be talking to? I have an Office Depot card.

Respectfully,

Ted L. Nancy

EST **GTC** 1920

THE GENERAL TRADING COMPANY

24/03/97

T L Nancy Esq
560 No. Moorpark Road
Apt 236
Thousand Oaks
CA 91360
USA

Dear Mr Nancy

Thank you for your letter of the 18th March.

Unfortunately we do not stock the range of product you require; namely"Famished Dwarf Frozen Dinners."

Thank you for your interest in the General Trading Company. We enclose a copy of our latest catalogue.

Yours sincerely

pp Graham Little

Michael Macrae
Managing Director

144 SLOANE STREET
SLOANE SQUARE
LONDON SW1X 9BL
TELEPHONE 0171 730 0411,
FAX 0171 823 4624

DIRECTORS:
DAVID C PART OBE DL
GARY WHITE FCA
NOEL SANTRY
MICHAEL MACRAE
TIM PART

THE GENERAL TRADING COMPANY
(MAYFAIR) LIMITED
REGISTERED NUMBER
170751 (ENGLAND)

560 No Moorpark Rd. Apt #236
Thousand Oaks, CA 91360

Wedding Registry Department
MACY'S DEPARTMENT STORE
P.O. Box 52039
Phoenix, AZ 85072   Sep 25, 1998

Dear Macy's Wedding Registry Department:

I want to look up Clovis Delzebra who I believe is registered at
your store for her wedding. I need bridal information: Gift
selections and table settings.

I want to get her Turtle Holes. I don't know the company name but
I believe the slogan is: "If you like Donut Holes then you'll
love Turtle Holes. Dee-licious! Try 'em with Jimmies."

Turtle Holes make a great wedding gift. Give her turtle holes.

<u>WEDDING GIFT LIST</u>
1st year - Paper
5th year - Diamonds
7th year - Onyx
10th year - Fudge
27th Year - Turtle Holes
30th year - Rope
50th year - More Turtle Holes (Hey, if something's good
                                you keep giving it)

I also may want frog slices with Brian Dennehy sauce. (The Tahini
poppyseed flavor, please) I believe you have the 16 ounce gift
tin. These are for myself. Scrumptious!

Please tell me who I would contact in the wedding registry
department to buy for Clovis Delzebra. I look forward to your
reply. Your store has always had the best customer service.
That's why I order from there.

Sincerely,

Ted L. Nancy
Ted L. Nancy

macy☆s west

October 14, 1998

Mr. Ted L. Nancy
560 No Moorpark Road Apt.#236
Thousand Oaks, CA 91360

Dear Mr. Nancy:

Thank you for your letter directed to our Bridal Registry department. Since this office is responsible for customer service, I have been asked to respond.

Please accept our apologies for any inconvenience you may have experienced regarding your recent Bridal inquiry. We appreciated your bringing this matter to our attention. Your comments and concerns are valuable to us.

Unfortunately, we are unable to locate a registry for Clovis Delzebra, or locate the items you have requested. Please be assured that Macy*s strives to maintain the highest level of customer service, and we hope you will accept our sincere apology for any frustration or inconvenience this may have caused you.

Mr. Nancy, again, thank you for writing and for being a valued Macy*s customer. If I may be of any additional assistance, please do not hesitate to contact me.

Sincerely,

Heather Biggs
Supervisor
Macy*s West Bridal & Gift Registry
(602) 929-3796

560 No. Moorpark Rd. Apt #236
Thousand Oaks, CA 91360   USA

Apr 16, 1999

FIJI VISITORS BUREAU
5777 W Century Blvd., Suite 220
Los Angeles, CA 90045

Dear Fiji Visitors Office,

MY SECOND LETTER!!!   PLEASE ANSWER ME!!!! In a world where
everyone complains, I want to stop complaining and single out the
good people of your Smron Store in Fiji. I was visiting the store
a few months ago in Fiji and they helped me out in a BIG way.

I became stuck in their air conditioner vent. I was really
squished up in there tight. My head, leg, torso, sandal,
everything was stuck up inside there. I don't know how I even got
there. The fine folks at Smron helped me up and out. They really
worked on me a while but they did it with a rope, shoe horn, and
some floor wax. Finally I was freed.

Please thank Smrons for me. This is a store that really cares
about their customers and not so much about their shoe horn. I
bought a coconut head! It's on my wall now. It looks at me.

Please write me and let me know that you got this letter and they
were thanked. It is VERY IMPORTANT to me. They really deserve
it, these people at Smron. I really appreciate hearing from you.

Also, if the dollar is worth a hundred pennies in the U.S. what is
it worth in Fiji? Thank you for helping me.

Sincerely,

Ted L. Nancy
Ted L. Nancy

fiji

ISLANDS

FIJI VISITORS BUREAU

5777 WEST CENTURY BVD
SUITE 220
LOS ANGELES
CALIFORNIA 90045
TELEPHONE
(310) 568-1616
FACSIMILE
(310) 670-2318

April 23, 1999

Ted L. Nancy
560 No. Moorpark Road #236
Thousand Oaks, CA 91360

Bula Mr. Nancy!

Thank you for your letter of April 16th which was received last April 22nd.

We are unable to thank Smron Store for you as we don't know of this named store doing business in Fiji.

Can you please provide us with more details of your accident such as when and where in Fiji this occurred? If you have the receipt of your purchase, maybe that will help us locate exactly which store you are referring to.

Regarding your query on the worth of the Fijian dollars in US – one gets about $1.50 Fijian dollar to 1 US dollar.

Hoping to hear from you soon, I remain

Sincerely yours,

Jo Tuamoto
Regional Director, The Americas

/lrw

560 No Moorpark Rd. Apt #236
Thousand Oaks, CA 91360 USA

Jo Tuamoto
Regional Director, The Americas
FIJI VISITORS BUREAU
5777 W. Century Blvd. Suite 220
Los Angeles, CA 90045   May 10, 1999

Bula Jo Tuamoto!

Thank you for your letter of April 23 which was received April
22nd. Smron Store is located in Suva. Although it is now called
Flob Store. I bought a lot of smron from them over the years.
However, I think they now just sell flob. Their slogan is "Grab
some flob if we are out of smron." I was there and I bought Sugar
cane, cotton, ginger ale, and a picture of Danny Devito.

Then I had my accident. I was really squished inside their vent
for a good 45 minutes. The details you asked for: While in that
vent, I had a very bad itch. They relieved that itch. Having an
itch that you cannot get to can be very discomforting. That itch
was in a place that I could not extend my fingers to. Luckily
someone from the Smron/Flob store scratched it for me. I can give
you more details of that itch if you like.

Can they be singled out? What about a certificate? Fiji should
be proud of them. I made a noise this morning. Tonga is a fine
neighbor. I am fidgety from Fiji. I would like to have this
store thanked already; it has been a long time. Will you bathe my
shrimp? I may bestow a valuable gift to that store or your office
as a representative of Fiji. When mentioning gift refer to:
Stiffened Cinnamon.

Thank you for helping me. I look forward to hearing from you.
Also, if X can dig a 5 inch hole in 1 hour using 2 shovels how
long would it take Y to dig that same hole but 2 inches smaller
using 3 shovels?

Sincerely,

Ted L. Nancy
Ted L. Nancy

fiji
I S L A N D S

FIJI VISITORS BUREAU

5777 WEST CENTURY BVD
SUITE 220
LOS ANGELES
CALIFORNIA 90045
TELEPHONE
(213)568 1616
FACSIMILE
(213) 670 2318

MR. TED L. NANCY
560 No. Moorpark Road #236
Thousand Oaks, CA 91360

first class

91360-3760 0£

560 No. Moorpark Rd. #236
Thousand Oaks, CA 91360

Dec 4, 1996

Customer Service
AJAX CLEANSER
C/O Colgate Palmolive Co.
300 Park Ave.
New York, NY 10022

Dear Ajax,

I use your stain remover all the time. Sometimes on stains. My
problem:

I had a nasty stain. I rubbed and rubbed and rubbed it and
finally it came off. Now the stain is on my sponge and I can't
get the stain off my sponge. It's a nasty stain.

How can I get this stain off my sponge? People refuse to eat with
this sponge in full view of them.

Hey, can Ajax be used in the hair? I thought it could but want to
talk to you before I sprinkle it on myself. I have a stain there
too. Thanks for writing and letting me know about:

A. My hair
2. Sponge Stain

Sincerely,

Ted L. Nancy

**COLGATE-PALMOLIVE** *COMPANY*
A Delaware Corporation

300 Park Avenue
New York, NY 10022-7499
Household Products
800-338-8388
Personal Care Products
800-221-4607

Consumer Affairs Department

December 26, 1996

Mr Ted L Nancy
560 N Moorpark Rd #236
Thousand Oaks, CA 91360

Dear Mr Nancy:

Thank you for your recent inquiry about Ajax Cleanser. We appreciate
your interest in our company and are pleased to have the opportunity to
respond.

Our company tests all of its products extensively to be sure they
provide consumer satisfaction when used for the purposes described on
the label. Sometimes, consumers report that they have had good results
using a product in other situations. The product warranty, however, is
limited to the uses described on the label.

We appreciate your taking the time to contact us. Please accept the
enclosed with our compliments.

Sincerely,

Barbara C. Myers
Consumer Affairs Representative
Consumer Affairs

TBM/nal

Enclosure
1009523A

 Recycled Paper

560 No. Moorpark Rd. #236
Thousand Oaks, CA 91360   USA

Stadium Events Director
LOUISIANA SUPERDOME
Sugar Bowl Dr.
New Orleans, LA 70112   Oct 8, 1998

Dear Stadium Events Director, Louisiana Superdome,

I have enjoyed your shows for many years. I was told to contact
you. That you would be VERY interested in seeing a tape of my
act. I perform at all festivals, fairs, and stadium events.

I am "Bob Ott The Aqua Tot." I am a 57 year old white male
(220 pounds). I wear a bathing suit and an adult holds me around
the waist as I splash around the shallow end of a swimming pool
like a child. I splash real good! We both circle the shallow end
as I splash around. I am "Bob Ott The Aqua Tot. I'm Hot!" I
have this on all posters and car window flyers.

I do an act that is 2 hours and 25 minutes but with the longer
show you get 45 minutes of more splashing. The crowd goes wild,
dogs bark! Yesterday I rubbed up against some tile. My swim
trunks balloon up in the water but you can't see anything. This
is set up through Gigante Lunchtime Performances.

After I come out of the pool I stand on the field in a wet swim
suit and cry while the adult quiets me with a toy. I cry for 85
minutes until the adult calms me with a puppet. But with the
longer show you get 15 more minutes of crying. This is some show!
I am Bob Ott The Aqua Tot!

Please direct me as to where I send my tape. I am interested in
joining your half time show. When the sparklers go off in the
pool it is wild. People scurry. But I just splash around as an
adult holds me by the waist and we circle the shallow end while my
trunks balloon up. I look forward to hearing from you soon.
Thank you, Louisiana Superdome. Where should I send my tape and
picture to?

Also, can you tell me how I get season tickets to your football
teams games? Thnak you. Send me info.

Sincerely,
Ted L. Nancy

SUGAR BOWL DRIVE

NEW ORLEANS, LA 70112

Alan S. Raphael
Marketing Manager

(504) 587-3858

(504) 587-3848 FAX

October 19, 1998

Mr. Ted L. Nancy
560 N. Moorpark Road # 236
Thousand Oaks, CA   91360

Dear Mr. Nancy:

As Marketing Director for the Louisiana Superdome, I am in receipt of
your letter dated October 8, 1998. I am indeed interested in finding out
more about your act and viewing your tape.

A new 20,000 seat arena is presently under construction adjacent to the
Louisiana Superdome. Perhaps some of the grand opening activities might
provide an excellent opportunity to showcase your talents.

Please forward any press materials and your video tape to me at the
Louisiana Superdome. We always have an eye out for new and unusual
talent. Thank you very much for your inquiry!

Sincerely,

Alan Raphael
Marketing Manager

http://www.superdome.com
E-Mail address:
raphael@superdome.com

AN SMG MANAGED FACILITY

560 No. Moorpark Rd. #236
Thousand Oaks, CA 91360

Nov 20, 1996

HEAD HERMIT
CAMALDOLSE HERMITS
IMMACULATE HEART HERMITAGE
Big Sur, California
93920-9656

Dear Chief Hermit:

Your fruitcake is terrific. I love walnuts! Where can I get
more? I have had 31 pieces and I don't feel so good. I belched
up a chunk of pineapple. There is pineapple in your cake, right?

Hey what about me? Do I count?

I would like to compliment everyone there involved in this
fantastic fruitcake. Some of the best fruitcake I have ever
belched up. You people are doing a good job with this cake.

Does anyone there want a back rub? How about a neck rub? I like
you. I'd like to be a hermit.

Where can I buy a ton of this stuff? Let me know and I'll eat it
up. I like hermit clothing.

Sincerely,

Ted L. Nancy

Future Hermit

Hermitage Bakery
CAMALDOLESE BENEDICTINE MONKS
IMMACULATE HEART HERMITAGE
BIG SUR, CALIFORNIA 93920-9656

Date-Nut Cake

We blend choice dates and fresh walnuts with a variety of rich spices, then dip the cake in brandy and age it to perfection.

2 ¼ lbs. $19.00

Fruitcake

We make this cake with the finest ingredients: cherries, pineapples, California raisins, walnuts, dates and Georgia pecans. Brandied and aged.

3 lbs. $19.00

Twin Pack

One date-nut cake and one fruitcake packaged together. (Count as two cakes when computing shipping charges.) No substitutes, please.

$36.00

Now four ways to order!

- **Mail** your order to the above address. (Check, VISA or MasterCard.)
- **e-mail** your order to monks@contemplation.com (VISA or MasterCard)
- **FAX** your order to (408) 667-0209   (VISA or MasterCard)
- **Call the toll-free bakery order line 1-800-826-3740** (VISA or MasterCard)
  (Please complete order form and have credit card handy before calling)

> Expedite UPS delivery; use street addresses; avoid P.O. boxes, Rural Route numbers, etc., if possible.
> In order that we may better serve you, please type or print all information. Sorry, no CODs.

BUYERS NAME AND ADDRESS

NAME _____

ADDRESS _____

_____

CITY, STATE, ZIP _____

TELEPHONE (   ) _____

SHIP TO BUYER AT ABOVE ADDRESS
(List gift orders on other side)

_____	Fruitcake @ $19.00	=$ _____
_____	Date-nut cake @$19.00	=$ _____
_____	TWIN PACK @ $36.00	=$ _____
_____	SHIPPING (from chart)	=$ _____
_____	Total	=$ _____

SHIP TO ARRIVE

_____ Now _____ Thanksgiving _____ Christmas

Other Date (specify) _____

GIFT ORDERS ON OTHER SIDE

Greeting is printed on shipping label.
Make sure recipient knows who is sending the gift!

METHOD OF PAYMENT

❏ CHECK ENCLOSED

❏ VISA   ❏ MASTERCARD

ACCOUNT NUMBER

EXPIRATION DATE   MO   YEAR

$ _____ + $ _____ = $ _____

PERSONAL   GIFT   GRAND
ORDER   ORDERS   TOTAL

SHIPPING CHARGES				
Number of Cakes to same address:				
	1 cake	2 cakes	3-4 cakes	5 or more
California	4.50	5.00	6.00	6.00
Outside California	6.00	7.00	10.00	11.00
Alaska & Hawaii	6.50	10.00	12.50	13.50
Canada	11.00	15.00	23.00	25.00
Other Countries	15.00	21.00	33.00	38.50

560 No. Moorpark Rd. #236
Thousand Oaks, CA 91360

Office Manager
GOODYEAR TIRE & RUBBER CO.
1144 E. Market St.
Akron, OH 44316   Feb 7, 1998

Dear Goodyear Tire & Rubber Company,

I am confirming my appearance at your Goodyear Tire & Rubber
Company headquarters for Friday, March 20, 1998 at one o'clock in
the afternoon. Please reply and let me know that I have the
correct information. This was set up with your special services
division through Gigante Lunch Performances.

I am "Nabar." I come to your office and let your employees drive
nails into me. I can take it! I come to your place of business
during the lunch break and let your employees hammer sixty five
nails into my sides and back. No stomach or I will bleed.
Employees love it and it is a morale builder. They talk about my
show for days. (Coffee break performance also available; I cannot
drink liquids for at least 45 minutes after show) My show brings
morale building atmosphere to the workplace. I never wince or
grimace. Once I blurted something that was mistaken as rude. But
that won't happen again. I am Nabar and like a good Nabar I want
to be there!

Please confirm my March 20 appearance at your Goodyear Tire &
Rubber Company headquarters. When I show up with my 9 trucks who
do I speak to?   Thank you.

Sincerely,

Ted L. Nancy
"Nabar, Hammer Nails Into Me"

March 12, 1998

Ted L Nancy
560 No. Moorpark Rd. #236
Thousand Oaks, CA 91360

Dear Sir:

Regarding your letter referencing a scheduled appearance at 1:00 PM on March 20, 1998 at the corporate headquarters facility of The Goodyear Tire & Rubber Company in Akron, Ohio, this letter is to advise you that no one at this location is aware of your performance that day and you should cancel this part of your schedule.

Wayne Matuch
Chief of Police
The Goodyear Tire & Rubber Co
(330) 796-4063

GOODYEAR

AKRON, OHIO 44316-0001

CERTIFIED

P 134 855 882

MAIL

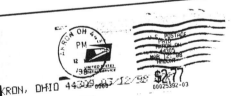

$2.77

MR TED L. NANCY
560 N Moorpark Rd #236
Thousand Oaks, CA 91360

RETURN RECEIPT
REQUESTED

560 No. Moorpark Rd. #236
Thousand Oaks, CA 91360

Mr. Wayne Matuch
Chief Of Police
GOODYEAR TIRE AND RUBBER
1144 E. Market St.
Akron, Ohio 44316   Apr 9, 1998

Dear Mr. Matuch,

Thank you so very much for getting back to me regarding my free
show at your Good Year Tire & Rubber Company headquarters. Yes,
there has been a mistake.

I was mistaken.   My show was not for March 20th and it was not
for your employees to hammer nails into me. This was for May 20th
and it was for your employees to drop a bowling ball on my head.
Your employees stand on a roof and they drop bowling balls
squarely onto my head. Only 31 employees please.   After 31 balls
on my head I get woozy (Speckled bowling balls only!)

This is a morale builder and a stress reducer. Employees feel
good about themselves and I get a bowling ball dropped on my head.
Everyone benefits. I am Nabar!

This is a FREE SHOW. It was set up through Gigante Lunchtime
Performances. You may know them by their motto: "Whether it's
getting nails hammered into you, or bowling balls dropped on your
head, or rakes up your nose, if it's done at lunchtime - it's
Gigante!" (Except Lubells)

Please confirm my May 20th appearance for 1:00 P.M. at your Good
Year Tire & Rubber facility in Akron, Ohio. I am Nabar and like a
good neighbor I am there! And once again I look forward to this
performance. Line up your employees and their bowling balls on
the roof and let them drop them on me.

Sincerely,

Ted L. Nancy
"Nabar, Drop Bowling Balls On Me"

FLOTSAM

"A Gentleman Never Interrupts"
Angelo Poofo

560 No. Moorpark Rd. #236
Thousand Oaks, CA 91360

Buyer
K MART DEPARTMENT STORES
3100 W Big Beaver Rd.
Troy, MI 48084   Dec 1, 1997

Dear K Mart:

I have invented a male underpants liner. Never change your
underwear again! This liner fits right in your shorts and can be
thrown away after 15 weeks. I have been wearing the same pair of
underwear for 105 days now and although they feel a little
stretchy they are perfectly clean. (A few hairs will fall off).

My liner is called "Underwear That's Fun To Wear!" It will be
sold exclusively in gas station snack shops and big and tall men
vending machines and finer Department Stores

With "Underwear That's Fun To Wear!" you only have to dispose of
the liner after a few months. And they come in five different
odors. Pine, lemon, cherry, glart, and new car.

I was told that K Mart - possibly the finest Department Store
there is - would like to see a sample of my underwear liners. How
can I arrange for you to look at this?

I look forward to hearing from you soon, Let's get this product
in your store in time for President's Day - a big underwear
shopping day.

Respectfully,

Ted L. Nancy

Kmart Corporation
International Headquarters
3100 West Big Beaver Road
Troy MI 48084-3163

January 27, 1998

TED L NANCY
#236
560 N MOORPARK RD
THOUSAND OAKS CA 91360

Dear Mr. Nancy:

Thank you for your recent information and interest in our corporation.

After careful consideration, it has been determined that we are unable to include your merchandise in our assortment. At this time, it has been decided that there is no mass market need for your liner. Therefore, the buyers have expressed no further interest in the offer presented.

We appreciate your thinking of Kmart and wish you success in placing your product.

Sincerely,

Richard Cozart
Supplier Diversity Department
248/643-5238

BURGE SCHOOL OF NURSING & TIRE SALES
" We Sell Tires - Not a Medical Facility"

560 No Moorpark Road #236
Thousand Oaks, CA 91360

Administrative Decisions
BURGE SCHOOL OF NURSING
1423 No Jefferson Ave.
Springfield, MO 65802   Sep 4, 1999

Dear Burge School Of Nursing,

I am opening my new business soon and want to call it the Burge
School Of Nursing & Tire Sales. We sell tires. We are not a
medical facility. We have no medical affiliations. We do not
treat patients. We sell car tires and truck rims.

Will this interfere with your Burge School Of Nursing name?   We
have monster wheels. Come see us for radials. Yes, we have VW
tires!

We offer no medical schooling or care. We have no in-patent or
out-patient services. We are not a clinic. We treat no one
medically. We sell no gauze or salves, remove no stitches. We do
not teach anyone how do diagnose a bad shin. We simply sell
automobile and SUV tires.

We don't think the similar names will be confusing. BUT if you
want me to change the name of my business to something else I
will. We are opening soon on the same street as you and want to
blend in. Changing our name is not a problem. Just let me know.

I look forward to hearing from you soon.

Sincerely,

Ted L. Nancy
President, Burge School Of Nursing & Tire Sales

COX
HEALTH SYSTEMS

Cox South
3801 S. National Ave.
Springfield, MO 65807
417/269-6000

Cox Walnut Lawn
1000 E. Walnut Lawn
Springfield, MO 65807
417/882-4700

Cox North
1423 N. Jefferson Ave.
Springfield, MO 65802
417/269-3000

Cox Monett
801 N. Lincoln
Monett, MO 65708
417/235-3144

Burrell Behavioral Health
1300 Bradford Parkway
Springfield, MO 65804
417/269-5400

Ferrell-Duncan Clinic
1001 E. Primrose
Springfield, MO 65807
417/881-1100

Oxford HealthCare
3660 S. National Ave.
Springfield, MO 65807
417/883-7500

Home Parenteral Services
2040 W. Vista
Springfield, MO 65807
417/887-7525

Primrose Place
1115 E. Primrose
Springfield, MO 65807
417/883-1546

Regional Services
3800 S. National Ave., Suite 540
Springfield, MO 65807
417/269-4343

October 4, 1999

Ted L. Nancy
President
Burge School of Nursing and Tire Sales
560 N. Moorpark Rd. #236
Thousand Oaks, CA 91360

Dear Mr. Nancy:

Thank you for your letter. As the Burge School of Nursing we have worked hard to make this name one was can be proud of.

Therefore, your use of this name is not one the organization can consent to allow you to use.

Very Truly Yours,

Lee Penninger, Esquire
In-house Counsel
Cox Health Systems

/dp

TedNancy092799

560 No. Moorpark Rd. #236
Thousand Oaks, CA 91360

Special Orders Dept.
KING BAGS
1500 Spring Lawn Ave
Cincinnati, Ohio 45223   Oct 5, 1999

Dear King Bags,

You have been highly recommended as one who I can order specialty
bags from with our slogans and picture on it.

I manufacture "Captain Reedys Cushion Crunch". These are snacks
that you find that have fallen in your cushion all crunched
together to make 1 large glazed snack. Eat it while you watch TV
on your couch. The following crumbs are included in Cushion
Crunch: Fritos, Doritos, Brachs candies, popcorn, squirrel hairs,
apples, ox jerky, cashews, poppyseeds, all together in a trail
like solid crumb mix piece. Each one is different depending on
what we find in the cushion. Our slogan: "We make more when more
falls in."

They are sold in a decorative gift tin with:

"Captain Reedys Slipcover Slop". This is what falls on your
slipcover while you are eating including: Pasta sauce, orange
juice, hot dog relish, egg yolk, gravy, squirrel foot, jam, Cheese
Whiz, all mixed in on your slipcover. Our slogan: "We make more
when more drips on you."

I would like bags made with our slogans and picture on them.
Perhaps you can suggest something: large bags, small bags,
reusuable bags, blue flannel bags, etc. that we could buy. We
need many.

Please direct me to the proper person (s) regarding ordering large
amounts of specialty bags from you.

Thank you,

Ted L. Nancy

"royalty of bags"

KING BAG & MANUFACTURING CO.
1500 spring lawn avenue / cincinnati, ohio 45223-1699/(513) 541-5440
Fax (513)541-6555

12 October 1999

Mr. Ted L. Nancy
560 No Moorpark Road #236
Thousand Oaks, CA 91360

Dear Ted:

Thank you for your recent request for bags for your "CAPTAIN REEDYS CUSHION CRUNCH". It sounds like a very unique product. I would think you could establish franchises for this product all over the U.S. Different areas of the country could offer local flavors, i.e. Cajun, marinated, extra crispy, etc. People could try selections from far away places.

When your product is consumed by the masses, and falls in the cushions, will you offer a re-cycled version? Perhaps you could call it "CAPTAIN REEDYS CUSHION CRUNCH II".

Ted, we can offer you whatever you need in bags. Our slogan is - "Tell us what you want and we will make it for you".

You might want to print on each bag - "The product that people have been sitting at home and waiting for" or "Try our product and see if you recognize anything".

With our bags and ideas you won't go wrong. Of course, our prices might be higher than any of the ordinary bag companies, but you will want a special company and that is what we are.

I look forward to working with you.

Very Truly Yours,

KING BAG AND MANUFACTURING COMPANY

John A. King

JAK/mo

■ sewn products for industry
■ bulk handling bags
■ route bags - job bags
■ welding curtains & blankets
■ textile bags - speciality bags
■ tarpaulins & custom covers
■ filter media
■ contractors supplies
■ nursery squares - allied products

560 No. Moorpark Rd.
Apt #236
Thousand Oaks, CA 91360

Sep 26, 1999

Customer Help
SAFEWAY SUPERMARKET
905 1st St
Gilroy, CA 95020

Dear Safeway Supermarkets,

Do you sell loose poppyseeds? I had heard that you did.

I need a just a few poppyseeds. Maybe 5 or 6. Do you have loose
ones? Let me know.

My friends in the Gilroy area shop at your store and they said
that if I wrote you I could order a few poppyseeds from you. Is
that true?

Thank you for answering me regarding my poppyseed problem.

Sincerely,

Ted L. Nancy

October 14, 1999

Ted L. Nancy
560 No. Moorpark Rd.
Thousand Oaks, CA 91360

Dear Ted L. Nancy,

Safeway does carry poppy seeds as a seasonal item. We usually get them around March, but they do not come loose. They come in packets which you should be able to find at any Safeway store with a floral department. Thank you for writing and I'm sorry that I could not help you more.

Sincerely,

Diana Pak

Diana Pak

560 North Moorpark Rd.
Apt #236
Thousand Oaks, CA 91360

Mar 6, 1998

Tourist Information
CITY OF HERMISTON
180 NE 2nd St.
Hermiston, OR 97838

Dear Hermiston Tourist Information,

Please tell me where I may locate one of your Shower Cap Vending
Machines throughout the city? I understand Hermiston has over 1
million Shower Cap Vending Machines placed throughout the city for
those that want to shower away from the home. I can't find them.
I travel to Hermiston 250,000 times a year and have only seen
three. Have they been removed? Also, do you still sell paper
slippers out of a tube at the Gas Company?

Please advise. Thank you. You have a lovely city. Great for
fresh baseboard trim. I love it! I look forward to hearing from
you.

Sincerely,

Ted L. Nancy
Ted L. Nancy

ADMINISTRATION
180 N.E. 2nd Street
Hermiston, OR 97838
(541) 567-5521
Fax (541) 567-5530
E-Mail Address:
hermcity@oregontrail.net

**COMMUNITY
DEVELOPMENT**
215 E. Gladys Avenue
Hermiston, OR 97838
(541) 564-0358
Fax (541) 567-6731

PLANNING
180 N.E. 2nd Street
Hermiston, OR 97838
(541) 567-5521
Fax (541) 567-5530
E-Mail Address:
planning@oregontrail.net

PUBLIC LIBRARY
235 E. Gladys Avenue
Hermiston, OR 97838
(541) 567-2882
Fax (541) 567-3551

**FIRE & EMERGENCY
SERVICES**
330 S. First Street
Hermiston, OR 97838
(541) 567-8822
Fax (541) 567-8469

POLICE
330 S. First Street
Hermiston, OR 97838
(541) 567-5519
Fax (541) 567-8469

MUNICIPAL COURT
330 S. First Street
Hermiston, OR 97838
(541) 567-6610
Fax (541) 567-8469

**WASTEWATER
TREATMENT**
2205 N. First Place
Hermiston, OR 97838
(541) 567-5272
Fax (541) 567-5200

June 2, 1998

Ted L. Nancy
560 N. Moorpark Road
Apt. #236
Thousand Oaks, CA 91360

Dear Mr. Nancy:

Your previous letter was received and forwarded over to the Chamber of Commerce. Evidently, they did not send a reply to you so, I will give you the information that I have.

1. There are no traveler's vending machines in the city of Hermiston.
2. Hermiston has a small bus stop which is housed in with another business.
3. There are no YMCA facilities in Hermiston.

If I can be of any further assistance, please let me know.

Sincerely,

Patricia Lynch
Senior Secretary

560 No. Moorpark Rd.
Apt #236
Thousand Oaks, CA 91360

Apr 2, 1999

Sales Dept.
BUICK MOTOR DIVISION
902 E Hamilton Ave.
Flint MI, 48505

Dear Buick,

I am very interested in your new Buick cars. I am particularly
looking for the Buick Popeye.

Please direct me to the dealer that sells the Buick Popeye. I am
a long time Buick driver. (When one Buick breaks down, I simply
buy another Buick. I've had 15 broken Buicks over the years). I
like the Popeye when I see it advertised on TV.

I look forward to hearing from you soon with my Popeye
information.

Buick is truly the finest car out there. I tell everyone that.
This morning I told my mailman about the Popeye as he stood there
in the hot sun stammering. He said he might get one too.

Thank you. Please send me info.

Sincerely,

Ted L. Nancy

Ted L. Nancy

BUICK

April 30, 1999

Mr. Ted L. Nancy
560 North Moorpark Road Apt. #236
Thousand Oaks, CA 91360

RE: 990041957

Dear Mr. Nancy:

Thank you for your letter of April 2, 1999 requesting information regarding a Buick Popeye. The information that you have obtained is inaccurate, Buick does not manufacture a vehicle by this name.

Unfortunately, Buick Motor Division has nothing available for distribution on this topic. Buick would be more than happy to send you brochures on our current models. Please feel free to contact Buick Customer Relations Center between 8:00-5:00 Monday through Friday, at 1-800-521-7300 if you are interested in these brochures.

Sincerely,

Yolanda A. Spencer

Yolanda A. Spencer
Customer Relations

560 No. Moorpark Rd. #236
Thousand Oaks, Ca. 91360

4/16/99

CURATOR, INTERNATIONAL SWIMMING HALL OF FAME
One Hall of Fame Dr.
Fort Lauderdale, FL. 33316

Dear Curator, Swimming Hall Of Fame,

I have developed a new swimming stroke. It was inspired by a
bloated blurp I watched cross a river.

I call it the "Quiver Stroke." My left hand is out of the water
(but moving) at all times. In fact, all fingers and toes are
constantly moving. One leg stays stiff and acts like a rudder.

I have a tape of me racing, doing the "Quiver Stroke." I beat
everyone. I win hands down. All because of this new stroke.
It's better then freestyle. World records will fall.

I want to patent my stroke. How do I do that? I have never seen
anyone swim like this. It will revolutionize man's relationship
with water. It's the "Fosbury Flop" of swimming. I am writing to
you because others in the swim community said you might help me.

Please help me. I need to patent my stroke so I can choose who
uses it. I look forward to hearing from you as soon as possible.
You can use it for free.

Very Sincerely,

Ted L. Nancy

Ted L. Nancy

June 3, 1999

Ted L. Nancy
560 North Moorpark Road, #236
Thousand Oaks, CA 91360

Dear Ted,

I received your letter in which you talk about your newly developed swimming stroke, the "Quiver Stroke". It sounds like a very unusual type of swimming and maybe of interest to alot of people.

In answer to your question, I have never heard of a stroke being patented for purposes of possession. The four competitive swimming strokes: freestyle, backstroke, breaststroke, butterfly are identified only by sets of rules which govern how they should legally be swam. If competing in a certified swimming race, the stroke must be legally performed or the participant is disqualified. None of these strokes belong to any person, place or organization.

If you wish to pursue the legality of this stroke, I can only suggest contacting a patent lawyer in your area.

If you desire you may send a photograph or video of you doing the stroke for our archives here at ISHOF.

I hope this has been of help and good luck with your project.

Sincerely,

Bob Duenkel
Executive Director

560 No Moorpark Rd. Suite #236
Thousand Oaks, CA 91360

Sep 3, 1999

Special Reservations dept.
CHRIS RUTHS STEAKHOUSE RESTAURANT
224 S Beverly Dr.
Beverly Hills, CA 90212

Hello Chris Ruths Restaurant,

I am Squiremaster of our club: Gum On Shoes.
We want to hold our twice weekly meetings at your restaurant. We
want to come every Tuesday and Friday night at 9:00 for 2 hours
and have food and drinks and discuss club business. Can we work
out a flat rate for the entire evening? There are 53 club
members. All will be eating and drinking.

Our club has gum on its shoes. We cross our legs and you can see
the gum stretch from our shoes to your floor. We put this gum on
our shoes before entering your restaurant. Then we walk in. The
gum sticks to the floor stretched from our shoe. When we lift our
foot. We will pay for ALL gum cleanup. (Up to a point).

Some of us are former semi nudists (wear shirt, socks, & shoes)
but that should not affect the gum on our shoe. We may want to
hold our nudist club meeting at your buffet. Please - let's avoid
splattering.

Please tell me how much to hold our first meeting which will be
Tuesday, Oct 19. Then we will come in again on Friday Oct 22. Or
we can hold it Monday and Thursday or Sunday and Wednesday. The
days are up to you.

Please advise on how much, and how much of a deposit you will need
for the 53 shoe & gum club members to eat and drink at your
restaurant. Thank you. I look forward to hearing from you soon
with deposit info.

Sincerely,

Ted L. Nancy
Squiremaster

RUTH'S STEAK HOUSE

224 South Beverly Drive
Beverly Hills, CA 90212
Phone 310.859.8744
Fax 310.859.2576
www.beverlyhills@ruthschris.com

September 10, 1999

Mr. Nancy,

Thank you for your recent letter regarding banquet facilities at the Beverly Hills Ruth's Chris Steak House. While we do not a flat rate for any functions here I can tell you how the pricing works. We average $50 per person, so a good rule of thumb would be $50 per person times 53 guests. This equals $2650. Note that this amount does not include any applicable sales tax or gratuity. Regarding the number of guests in your group I have to inform you that our private dining room will hold an maximum of 40 people.

On the subject of nudity, we do have a dress code. Our dress code requires our guests to be fully clothed. As we are not a "clothing optional" facility we would require that all of the members of your group be fully clothed at all times. This it would seem would render the "splattering" issue moot.

Our private dining room is available Sunday through Thursday nights. While it is possible to book the room at 9pm at night please be advised that our kitchen closes at 10pm and the bar at 11pm. We will require a $300 deposit (cash or money order) deposit is non refundable should the function cancel within 72 hours of the booking.
In regard to the "gum" issue, please budget $200 for each function you wish to hold at the restaurant.
Thank you again for your interest and please call me personally with any questions or concerns.

Sincerely,

Nicholas Kolen
General Manager

560 No. Moorpark Rd. #236
Thousand Oaks, CA 91360

Jan 22, 1998

Park Services
KLONDIKE GOLDRUSH NATIONAL PARK
117 South Maine
Seattle, WA 98104

Dear Customer Services Dept.:

As part of my experiment on the study of bears, I would like to
come to Klondike National Park in my Grizzly bear suit and live
with the bears for 3 days. This is a realistic looking bear suit
and has fooled many including my postman. This study involves me
living with the grizzlies to see how they behave. I have done
this experiment before with cows. And nothing happened!

I will enter the park in my bear suit and go right to the bears.
I will sit down with them and start eating. I will be properly
scented. I want to record how the bears share the food. This is
for my experiment! (A paper will be written) If a bear waves
"hello" it's probably me.

Please let me know how I may obtain permission for my analysis
with these bears. (Worked with Kodiak before in Melford; named
Randy.) Who would I contact to secure permission? This is a much
needed study. I eagerly await your response.

Sincerely,

Ted L. Nancy

United States Department of the Interior

NATIONAL PARK SERVICE
Klondike Gold Rush
National Historical Park
Seattle Unit
117 South Main Street
Seattle, Washington 98104

IN REPLY REFER TO

N22(KLSE)

Mr. Ted L. Nancy
560 North Moorpark Road, #236
Thousand Oaks, California 91360

February 1, 1998

Dear Mr. Nancy;

Thank you for your letter of January 22, 1998, in which you inquired about the possibility of coming to Klondike Gold Rush NHP-Seattle Unit to observe the bears.

We appreciate your interest in this park and especially your interest in wildlife. However, we have no bears in this National Park Service site. We are an urban, cultural resource park.

Good luck on your bear study, and I would suggest a more cautious approach to studying bears than to just suit up and join the bears. Bears are very dangerous animals and should only be near us when we are completely protected and at a safe distance. When I was a young boy an old hunter once told me that when people make a 'mistake' with a bear, the bear makes a 'steak' of the people. I have found that statement to be a great reminder to me whenever I plan to go near bears.

Again, good luck in your studies of bears.

Sincerely,

Willie Russell, Superintendent
Klondike Gold Rush NHP-Seattle Unit

Enclosures(2)

560 No. Moorpark Rd. #236
Thousand Oaks, CA 91360

Jan 26, 1998

City Employment Dept.
CITY OF CLOVIS
1033 5th St.
Clovis, CA 93612

Dear City Employment Dept.:

I am a noise expert. I am seeking employment in Clovis as a noise
and clamor expert. I can distinguish most noises (up to 502
types. I have trouble with boxes falling).

I understand you are looking for a Level 5, B1, Sound and Pitch,
QR17 Noise Expert in your city to explain noises.

I can distinguish both outside and inside noises. (I have trouble
with dishes breaking). I am a semi-expert on indoor noises
involving wood sounds, buzzing, books being dropped and shoe
scrapings.

Please tell me how I may apply for this position? I can relocate
upon needed.

I look forward to your reply. Thank you. Clovis is truly the
city of many varied noises. I look forward to a long employment
there. Thank you.

Sincerely,

Ted L. Nancy

Ted L. Nancy

CITY OF CLOVIS

CITY HALL • 1033 FIFTH STREET • CLOVIS, CA 93612

February 11, 1998

Ted L. Nancy
560 N. Moorpark Rd. #236
Thousand Oaks CA   91360

Dear Mr. Nancy,

We received your letter date Jan. 26, 1998 concerning interest in a Level 5, B1, Sound and Pitch, QR17 Noise Expert. I regret to inform you that the City of Clovis is not looking for someone for that position nor do we have that position. We currently have a few Part Time positions available and if you would like more information on them you can call our Job Line at (209)297-2329.

Thank you for your interest in employment with the City of Clovis.

Sincerely,

Amanda Campbell
Amanda Campbell

560 No. Moorpark Rd.
Apt #236
Thousand Oaks, CA 91360

Jul 27, 1999

BETTER BUSINESS BUREAU DES MOINES
505 5th Ave.
Suite 950
Des Moines, Iowa 50309

Dear Better Business Bureau:

I want to know where your "Smells Like Salad" restaurants are
located. I know you have 12,003 of them in your city. Yet I have
only seen one and I can't remember where. There is nothing like
the smell of salad from 20 feet away. I once smelled a radish on
someone's shirt. Call me Enrique for an hour when we first meet.

I became disoriented in your city and have never been able to find
this "Smells Like Salad" restaurant again. I like walnuts! If
you hear someone yell out 'Hey, Bernardo' when they first meet
me – disregard that person and continue to call me Lorie.

So...can you help me?

I have enjoyed Des Moines and its restaurants for years. Perhaps
these restaurants now go under a different name. Do you have a
list of some of your fine restaurants that I could write to and
see if they are indeed the "Smells Like Salad" restaurants that I
remember growing up with?

I look forward to hearing from you. Des Moines is a wonderful
place for salad mixins. Thank you.

Sincerely,

Ted L. Nancy
Ret.

August 20, 1999

Mr. Ted L. Nancy
560 No. Moorpark Rd.
Apt. 236
Thousand Oaks, CA 91360

RE: "Smells Like Salad"

Dear Mr. Nancy:

Thank you for contacting the Better Business Bureau with your inquiry. I searched our database for information on a restaurant by the name of Smells Like Salad and found nothing. Since we have no information in our system on that company name, I am enclosing a list of restaurants in our city that is published weekly in *The Des Moines Register*.

I hope this list will be helpful to you in your search for Smells Like Salad.

Sincerely,

Amy Merrill
Consumer Representative

560 No. Moorpark Rd.
Apt 236
Thousand Oaks, CA 91360

Apr 2, 1999

Curator
VALLEY FORGE HISTORICAL SOCIETY MUSEUM
Rte. 23
Valley Forge, PA 19481

Dear Valley Forge Historical Museum

I understand you have the exhibit ROAD RAGE PICTURES on display at
your museum.

How wonderful! I also understand that you are seeking photos for
this exhibit. I have the following ROAD RAGE photos which I would
like to offer your museum. They are from my own collection. I
offer them now to you:

Cursing at foreigners
Shoot the finger
Blurry sports van
Semi attractive girl giving the bird
Changing tire and getting sprayed by asphalt
Angry tiny man

I have shown this exhibit at many leading museums and would like a
permanent home for it. I believe your museum is perfect for this
fine collection. When is your exhibit running through and do I
have to wear a tie?

I understand that in April your museum hosts Valborgsmassoafton.
Is this true When in April? How much? Thank you for your help.
Do you want to see my museum quality Road Rage pictures?

I also have Boat Rage pictures and a Baby Carriage Rage photo.

Respectfully,

Ted L. Nancy

April 14, 1999

Ted L. Nancy
560 No. Moorpark Rd.
Thousand Oaks, CA 91360

Dear Mr. Nancy:

I am writing in regards to your letter of April 2, 1999 on a ROAD RAGE PICTURES exhibit. Unfortunately, you were misinformed. We do not have any such exhibit here at the Society. Our exhibits feature Valley Forge, the winter encampment of 1777-1778, George Washington, and the American Revolution. I am not familiar with an exhibit such as you mentioned.

The Valborgsmassoafton event is not hosted by us. You may be thinking of the American Swedish Historical Museum in Philadelphia. I do not have any information on their programs so you could contact them directly for details at (215) 389-1776 or by mail at 1900 Pattison Avenue, Philadelphia PA 19145.

Sincerely,

Stacey A. Swigart

Stacey A. Swigart
Curator

My Road Rage Collection

BLURRY SPORTS VAN

Getting Sprayed by Asphalt

ANGRY TINY MAN

SEMI ATTRACTIVE
GIRL GIVING THE BIRD

CURSING AT
FOREIGNERS

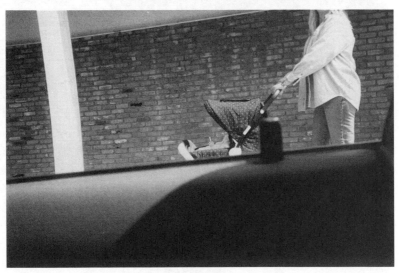

BABY Carriage Rage

PORTFOLIO

"I'm on the Dead End of a Pogo Stick"
My Dad at Breakfast

560 No. Moorpark Rd. #236
Thousand Oaks, CA 91360

Feb 9, 1997

Business Permits
CITY OF ALEXANDRIA
301 King St.
Alexandria, VA 22314

Dear Business Permits Dept.:

I want to apply for a business permit in your fine city. I have always admired Alexandria. You have great boar melts.

I operate the SOUP & SLEEP RESTAURANTS. You can either order soup or sleep. A hostess will greet you and you would say, "I'd like to sleep." She will lead you to a table where you can catch a few winks.

Or you might say, "I'd like some soup." She would then lead you to a table where you can have vegetable soup. (That's all we serve). We may have snooze booths, but I doubt it. You share tables so that you are having your soup while someone's asleep.

This is not to be confused with the NAP & SLURP restaurants. We are not affiliated with them in anyway.

Please let me know how I may operate my 291 restaurants in your beautiful city. I look forward to hearing from you soon. Good sippin' and a healthy sleep.

Respectfully,

Ted L. Nancy
President SOUP & SLEEP
Formally SLAW & SLUMBER RESTAURANTS

City of Alexandria, Virginia

Department of Finance
Revenue Administration Division
P. O. Box 178, Alexandria, Virginia 22313

Business Tax Branch
(703) 838-4680

Taxpayers Assistance Branch
(703) 838-4570

Personal Property Tax Branch
(703) 838-4560

April 24, 1997

Tax Enforcement Branch
(703) 838-4684

Mr. Ted L. Nancy, President
Soup & Sleep
560 North Moorpark Road #236
Thousand Oaks, CA 91360

Dear Mr. Nancy:

Thank you for your letter dated February 9, 1997, regarding the process for obtaining a City of Alexandria Business License to operate a Soup & Sleep Restaurant. The type of business you propose is a truly unique concept in Alexandria, or any other city, and more than one type of business license would be required. In order to obtain any business license in the City the following requirements must be met after your initial visit to the Business Tax Office:

1. You must obtain Zoning approval before conducting business in the City.

2. Code Enforcement Bureau must determine if your firm needs a Certificate of Occupancy or a Hazardous Use Permit (i.e. sleeping customers may be falling off chairs).

3. If your firm is incorporated, the Business Tax Branch needs a copy of your Certificate of Authority from the Virginia State Corporation Commission as well as a copy of your Articles of Incorporation.

In order to obtain a restaurant license the following requirements must be met:

1. You must obtain a City of Alexandria Health Permit. Since you plan to have some people sleeping at tables while others are eating the City Health Department may require some unusual sanitary precautions (i e. hairnets for all customers).

2. You must register with the City of Alexandria Meal Sales Tax Office.

3. If you will be serving alcoholic beverages Virginia ABC Licenses will be needed as well as additional City licenses (which may make the sleep aspect of your business popular with those customers who find that they have over indulged).

City of Alexandria, Virginia

Business Tax Branch
(703) 838-4680

Personal Property Tax Branch
(703) 838-4560

Department of Finance
Revenue Administration Division
P. O. Box 178, Alexandria, Virginia 22313

ALL-AMERICA CITY
1985
1964

Taxpayers Assistance Branch
(703) 838-4570

Tax Enforcement Branch
(703) 838-4684

Mr. Ted Nancy
April 23, 1997
Page 2

The requirements for obtaining a business license for the use of sleeping space in your restaurants will depend on several factors. For example, if you should choose to provide snooze booths you may be classified as a hotel and be subject to the City's transient lodging tax. Another factor would be exactly how long customers are permitted to sleep in your business. Will any customers be staying overnight or will they be permitted morning dozes and quick afternoon naps only? If any customers will be spending the night will you be providing a safe place for them to store personal belongings (i.e. wallets, watches, laptops,... etc.). If so, will you be charging for this service? We strongly suggest you have the Alexandria Police Department perform a background check on any local person you employ to administer this service. If showers will be provided it is important that you be aware that it is unlawful for two or more people to shower together in a public place (i.e. next to the people who are sleeping or eating soup) and a separate Health Permit may be required. Depending on the circumstances you may be classified as a personal service. You should also be aware that the unusual nature of this exciting new concept will probably necessitate a Special Use Permit from the Office of Planning and Zoning.

The City of Alexandria appreciates and welcomes exciting new business concepts and the Business Tax Branch is especially eager to be of assistance. We fully expect that your new establishments will be popular. If you have any questions or need any further assistance please do not hesitate to call us at (703) 838-4680 Monday through Friday from 8:00 AM to 5:00 PM.

Very Sincerely,

Gary G. Rossi
Business Tax Branch

REVENUE ADMINISTRATION DIVISION
Department of Finance
City of Alexandria
P O Box 178
Alexandria VA 22313

4/25/97

Forwarding & Address Correction Requested

Mr. Ted L. Nancy, President
Soup & Sleep
560 North Moorpark Road #236
Thousand Oaks, CA 91360

AUTO 91360

560 No. Moorpark Rd. #236
Thousand Oaks, CA 91360

Dec 1, 1997

Mall Management Office
MALL OF VICTOR VALLEY
14400 Bear Valley Rd.
Victorville, CA 92392

Dear Victor Valley Mall:

I want to operate my empty kiosk from your mall. My empty kiosk
is called: MALL NEEDS.

You do everything at my kiosk that you can't find to do elsewhere
in the mall. Stop by and tie your shoe. Throw away your trash.
Spank your kid. Throw out an empty Orange Julius cup. Read your
receipt. It's all here. Whatever you thought of doing in the
mall and waited to do because you couldn't find a place - you can
do at Mall Needs, my empty kiosk.

Never again stop just anywhere in the mall to yell at your kid,
check how much change you have, look at people, or adjust your
trousers

Please tell me how I go about operating my kiosk from you mall?
It's time for MALL NEEDS - Victorville's place to tuck your shirt
in.

I look forward to hearing from you soon regarding rental space
costs and where I will be located. Thank you very much.

Sincerely,

Ted L. Nancy

January 26, 1998

Ted L. Nancy
560 No. Moorpark Rd. Apt# 236
Thousand Oaks, CA 91360

Thank you for showing interest in the Specialty Leasing Program at The Mall of Victor Valley. The information below is required in order to give you a quote of cost to lease a store or kiosk at The Mall of Victor Valley.

Legal name of business, contact person's name, address, and phone number.
Business Plan:

    a. Projected Sales
    b. Projected Expenses
    c. Planned Changes
    d. Financials
    e. Business Experience
    f. Store Operating Philosophy

Photographs of existing store.
A detailed listing and photographs of products to be sold.
Price points of products.
Square footage required.
Length of lease.
Store signage drawings (to be approved by Mall Management).
Provide copy of sellers permit (not required at this time).
Provide copy of insurance with additional insured (not required at this time).
Provide copy of City of Victorville Business License (not required at this time).

After I receive the above information I will be able to provide you with a proposal for a lease at The Mall of Victor Valley.

Should you have any questions please contact me at (760) 241-3145.

I look forward to working with you in the future.

Sincerely,

THE MALL OF VICTOR VALLEY

Michael Scott Cummings
Specialty Leasing Representative

MSC

560 No. Moorpark Rd. Apt #236
Thousand Oaks, CA 91360

Registrar
STETSON UNIVERSITY
421 N. Woodland Blvd.
De Land, FL 32720   Dec 16, 1996

Dear Registrar,

I have heard that your center has a mascot college. And that you
train and place mascots at universities, colleges, professional
sports teams, and flag shops. I have always wanted to be a
mascot. I can do somersaults and cartwheels while I'm wearing
knights armor and I have performed as "THE SCREAMING SPONGE" and
"THE WHISTLING THERMOS." What do I need to do to get into your
professional mascot school? I have been a gorilla for a mattress
store. Heat doesn't bother me.

I have six toes. Four on one foot and two on the other. It
enables me to run quickly. I can run a perfect square faster than
anyone I know. (I have raced the Firestone Tire salesman).

As "THE SCREAMING SPONGE" I run into the stands and soak up any
spill yelling at the top of my lungs. As "THE WHISTLING THERMOS"
I toot sports tunes through my rubber stopper as I give out hot
coffee.

Please let me know when your classes start. And what the
education costs. Do you have co-ed dorms? I could come up with a
cheer for that. I think my GI Bill will pay for this.

Thank you, Stetson University. (I love your hats!). You are the
best school out there and certainly the best for mascots. That is
what I have been told by the "BELCHING HORSE." If I have not
reached the correct place can you please write and let me know?
I look forward to hearing from you soon with semester info.

Sincerely,

Ted L. Nancy

Ted L. Nancy

STETSON UNIVERSITY

Office of the Registrar
Campus Box 8298
DeLand, FL 32720 3773
(904) 822-7140

January 6, 1997

Mr. Ted L. Nancy
560 No. Moorpark Rd. Apt. #236
Thousand Oaks, CA 91360

Dear Mr. Nancy:

I am sorry to report that you have been misinformed by the "Belching Horse". Stetson University does not have a "mascot college" or even a "mascot major".

I personally don't know of any university that has such a program, although there may well be some. I do believe the Ringling Brothers Circus has a "clown college" which may be of interest to you.

I'm sorry I can't be more help to you. Good luck in your search.

Cordially,

A. L. Wehrle

Mr. A. L. Wehrle
University Registrar

ALW:tlr

560 No. Moorpark Rd. Apt #236
Thousand Oaks, CA 91360

Sep 12, 1998

Chief Of Staffing
OKLAHOMA DEPARTMENT OF CORRECTIONS
820 Manuel Ofc
Chandler, OK 74834

Dear Oklahoma Department Of Corrections:

I want to apply for a job with your government firm. I am ready
to guard someone. My height and weight is: 2 feet 1 inch, 65
pounds. I am a former international circus performer and glittery
sideshow attraction. You may have heard of me. I am
"Pip The Mighty Squeak." Now I want to guard prisoners in our
prison system. My height will work for me as I am able to hide in
drapes. I am very tiny.

Do not discount me. I can be valuable. I can hide in rolled up
carpeting. I am ready to protect and serve. I am Pip The Mighty
Squeak! I toured over 34 countries including Norway. I hid in a
jar once.

I am now ready to stand in front of our prisoners and make sure
everything is OK. I can be very, very important. I guarded a
parrot once and did a very good job. I can hide in a beard. (Oak
Ridge Boy type beard) I rented out "The Crow" many times.

Please send me an application form. I want to work there. I am
moving to Oklahoma soon. Thank you.

Sincerely,

Ted L. Nancy
Pip The Mighty Squeak

JAMES L. SAFFLE
DIRECTOR

FRANK KEATING
GOVERNOR

STATE OF OKLAHOMA
OKLAHOMA DEPARTMENT OF CORRECTIONS
DISTRICT III COMMUNITY CORRECTIONS

October 5, 1998

Ted L. Nancy
560 No. Moorpark Rd. Apt. #236
Thousand Oaks, Ca. 91360

Dear Ted

I am in receipt of your letter inquiring about employment opportunities with the Oklahoma Department of Corrections. In that we are an equal opportunity employer we welcome a person of your diverse experience and qualifications showing interest in what this field offers. We never discount anyone that can further their career and our mission from consideration for employment. Your abilities are quite astounding and I am sure that they can be used in this and/or many related fields within the state system. In that you didn't tell us exactly what position you are interested in pursuing we have taken the liberty of sending you an application form for testing for state employment. By completing this application and sending it to the address listed you will be eligible for testing in our many varying fields of service.

Again, thank you Ted for your interest and with your impending move, let me be the first Oklahoman to welcome Pip The Mighty Squeak to our state.

Sincerely,

Michael Dunkle, District Supervisor
District III Probation and Parole/Community Corrections

560 No. Moorpark Rd.
Suite #236
Thousand Oaks, CA 91360

Rentals Office
BYRDSVILLE SHOPPING CENTER
9869 Pulaski Pike
Toney, Alabama 35773   Apr 13, 1998

Dear Mall Rental Department:

Here is the service I wish to bring to your mall:
"Stop Smoking In My Car." You will quit the habit after 9 hours
in my car. And I can carry up to 5 passengers. Hop in and light
up. You will stop smoking after 3 rides. (I drive.)

When you leave my car after 9 hours in the parking lot with the
windows locked shut you will feel refreshed, pale, and ready to
get in your own car and drive home. And I give a certificate!
Your eyes may be bloodshot. I return for 2 follow up visits.
Although I may use my brother's car for that. (My own car gets
stale)

When your mate is shopping you go for a nice smoky drive in the
mall parking garage with 5 other people in my car. I circle the
garage approximately 568 times depending on size and foot traffic.
When you get out you don't want another cigarette for 8 days
(Average)

This is a much needed service! One Latvian fella said he can't
believe he ever smoked and continues to ask for rides. (Have on
my answering machine)

Please send me info for the use of your mall parking garage. I am
opening in the Toney area soon. What process do we need to go
through for me to operate my service in your parking garage?
Thank you. I look forward to my reply.

Sincerely,

Ted L. Nancy
Stop Smoking In My Car

July 28, 1998

Ted L. Nancy
560 N. MoorPark Road #236
Thousand Oaks, CA 91360

Dear Mr. Nancy:

　　Please allow me to introduce myself, I am Marshall Byrd, owner of Byrdsville Shopping Center, Toney, Alabama.

　　I received your letter today, July 28, 1998. Sorry but I did not receive your previous letter. It must have got lost in the mail.

　　We welcome your interest in opening your business in Byrdsville Shopping Center. Please advise as to the amount of space you will need and the parking space desired. We have Suite from 800 square feet to 7,500 square feet and park space, for 108 vehicles. Please advise the type of business you will operate.

　　Please call me at (256)828-1092 or fax me at (256)828-1126, for any desired information.

　　　　　　　　　　Sincerely yours,

　　　　　　　　　　Marshall Byrd

THE BIB BARN

"NOTHING ELSE BUT BIBS"

560 No. Moorpark Rd. #236
Thousand Oaks, CA 91360

Mr. Marshall Byrd
BYRDSVILLE SHOPPING CENTER
9869 Pulaski Pike #D
Toney, Alabama 35773   Sep 2, 1998

Dear Mr. Byrd:

I own the Bib Barn and I want to lease store space from you in
your mall. I need big amounts of space; lots of room. As much as
you can give me. We may have to break open 2 stores. Maybe more.
We are a BIG bib store. All we sell is bibs. We carry nothing
but bibs. That's it! Just bibs. That's all. I am interested in
becoming your anchor store at the end of the mall. Please tell me
what is available.

If it's bibs you want visit the Bib Barn. We DO NOT stock babies
bibs. We are currently out of lobster bibs. See us for all your
business bib needs. Including the 3 foot bib. (Out of green).
If it's suede bibs you're looking for see us third. Shop
elsewhere, get a price, use their restroom, ask questions, crunch
numbers, then see us for the best suede bibs in Alabama.

"We don't fib when it comes to bibs." Our sales managers are all
freckled. Yes we have the five foot bib. Covers everything. In
stock. We are not affiliated with the Bib Mart or the Bib
Superstore. We are not carrying dental bibs anymore. Browse our
bibs. "You can spend a day in our aisle."

Please send me information on what is available. Thank you. I
look forward to hearing from you soon.

Sincerely,

Ted L. Nancy

(205) 828-1126   Fax (205) 828-1126

9869 Suite D Pulaski Pike • Toney, AL 35773

September 21, 1998

Mr Ted L. Nancy
560 No.Moorpark Road # 236
Thousand Oaks, Ca. 91360

Dear Mr Nancy:

    I attempded to contact you by phone on Sep.19,1998, but I
could not find a number for BIB BARN or for Ted L. Nancy.The operator
could not find a listing.

    Please FAX me your phone number and fax , then I will call
you so we can discuss the amount of space and a price.

                         Sincerely Yours,

                         Marshall L Byrd

THE HANDKERCHIEF HUT

"ONLY HANDKERCHIEFS"

560 N. Moorpark Rd. #236
Thousand Oaks, CA 91360

Oct 5, 1998

Mr. Marshall Byrd
BYRDSVILLE SHOPPING CENTER
9869 Pulaski Pike
Toney, Alabama 35773

Dear Mr. Byrd:

Once again it was a pleasure to hear from you. I'm sure the Bib
Barn will be suitable at the north end of the mall as your anchor
store. Now for the south end of the mall. I was wondering if
you have space available for my business - The Handkerchief Hut.

This is your anchor hut at the other end of the mall. We are
very, very tiny: 3 feet wide and 7 feet high. Only 1 person can
fit in the hut at 1 time. When a customer comes in the clerk has
to leave. (He can hang out in the candle shop) There is just
enough room to move your elbow up and put a handkerchief in your
pocket. (Do NOT blow your nose in the hut; no room)

We have all handkerchief accessories. See us last, crunch
numbers, then buy from us. "In a rut? Then get your butt over
to the Hut." We have the 9 foot handkerchief. (Out of purple)

Let me know about prices for the rental. I look forward to
hearing from you soon.

Sincerely,

Ted L. Nancy

BYRDSVILLE SHOPPING CENTER
9965-9005 PULASKI PIKE.
TONEY, ALABAMA 35773
(205) 828-1126

FRIENDS DON'T
LET FRIENDS
DRIVE DRUNK

MAILED FROM ZIP CODE

Ted L. Nancy
560 N. Moorpark Road
Suite #236
Thousand Oaks, CA 91360

560 N. Moorpark Rd. Apt #236
Thousand Oaks, CA 91360

Mar 6, 1998

Tax Dept.
CITY OF GARDENA
1700 W 162nd St
Gardena, CA 90247

Dear Gardena Tax Office:

Please send me whatever info I need for my taxes regarding my
business. I have a business I want to set up in your city: My
business is:

I will go through your mail with you. When your mail comes call
me up and I will come over and we will go through your mail
together.

Never again do you have to go through your mail by yourself. Not
once. And I am cheaper then the other guy. I stop the drudgery
of you going through your mail alone. I will be there as you open
your mail, look at your bills, flyers, personal notes, magazines,
invitations, whatever. I will study them along with you, and
leave after you have put them away on your desk top. I WILL NOT
stay after this service is finished.

When my own bill comes in the mail a few weeks later I will go
through that with you too. And stay until you put it on your
desk.

Please send me tax info. Thank you. I look forward to my
application soon. (And so does my associate who is with me when
my own mail comes).

Sincerely,

Ted L. Nancy

DONALD L. DEAR, *Mayor*
MAS FUKAI, *Mayor Pro Tem*
STEVEN C. BRADFORD, *Councilmember*
JAMES W. CRAGIN, *Councilmember*
GWEN DUFFY, *Councilmember*

1700 WEST 162nd STREET / GARDENA, CALIFORNIA 90247-3778 / (310) 217-9500

CITY of GARDENA

MAY Y. DOI, *City Clerk*
LORENZO F. YBARRA, *City Treasurer*
MITCHELL G. LANSDELL, *City Manager*
LISA E. KRANITZ, *City Attorney*

March 11, 1998

Mr. Ted L. Nancy
560 N. Moorpark Rd., Apt. 236
Thousand Oaks, CA 91360

RE: Your request for a business license application

Dear Mr. Nancy:

Enclosed is the business license application form for the City of Gardena. All completed license applications for any business located within city limits need to be presented **IN PERSON.**

Zoning approval from the Community Development Department is required before a license can be issued. It is the applicant's responsibility to obtain this approval. **Personal contact** for this process is recommended.

Please contact Community Development at (310)217-9524, or the Business License Division at (310)217-9518 for any questions you may have concerning this matter.

Very truly yours,

Gert Watson
Gert Watson
Business License Inspector

enclosure

560 No. Moorpark Rd. #236
Thousand Oaks, CA 91360

Mar 16, 1998

Business Permits
CITY OF FEDERAL WAY
33530 1st Way S.
Federal Way, WA 98003

Dear Business Permits Department:

I am the owner of "THE CAPTAIN'S BAD NOISE SWIM CLUB." I need a
permit to operate a 250,000 gallon mobile pool on wheels. My
pickup truck is filled with water and I announce through my PA
system: "This is the Captain's Bad Noise Swim Club in your
neighborhood now. I am driving around. Come on in and splash
around. Grab your trunks and get in the back of my truck!!"

Please help me secure my permit so I can get this thing on the
streets. I have a filtering sytem. This is not filth water. I
look forward to hearing from you soon with my permit information
to operate my swimming truck that roams your streets with people
in it. Thank you. Soon I will be in your neighborhood. Do you
sell towels?

Sincerely,

Ted L. Nancy

CITY OF **FEDERAL WAY**

33530 1ST WAY SOUTH

(253) 661-4000
FEDERAL WAY, WA 98003-6210

Mr. Ted L. Nancy
560 North Moorpark Road, #236
Thousand Oaks, CA 91360

April 3, 1998

Re: *The Captain's Bad Noise Swim Club – Mobile Pool*

Dear Mr. Nancy:

Thank you for your letter of March 16, 1998, requesting permitting information for your mobile pool proposal. Your letter has been forwarded to me for response. In your letter you propose to operate a 250,000 gallon mobile pool using city streets to move from neighborhood to neighborhood.

A business such as you have described in your letter will require several issues be reviewed and certain permit approvals obtained before you might be permitted to operate. These include:

1) Preapplication zoning and public works review;
2) Right-of-way activity permit approval;
3) Traffic control plan;
4) Business registration approval; and,
5) Review and approval from the Seattle-King County Department of Public Health to operate a pool facility.

For your convenience, a business registration, right-of-way activity permit application, and master land use application have been enclosed. You can contact the Seattle-King County Department of Public Health by writing them at the Alder Square office. The address is 1404 Central Avenue, Suite 101, Kent, WA 98032. Their phone number is (206) 296-4708.

Please contact me if you have additional general questions concerning business registration and permitting. My phone number is (253) 661-4121.

Sincerely,

Martin Nordby, CCEO
Code Compliance Officer

enc

c: Greg Fewins, Principal Planner
      Ken Miller, Street Systems Manager
      Peg Buck, Accounting Technician

POOL.WPD

260 No. Moorpark Rd. Apt #236
Thousand Oaks, CA 91360

Sep 24, 1998

Jobs Dept.
SCAN HEALTH PLAN
PO Box 22616
Long Beach, CA 9

Dear Scan Health Plan Co.:

I want to apply for your job as a CLAMS MANAGER. I have managed clams a lot. And I have supervised clams that are managed. And they are in line. These clams don't get in trouble with my supervision.

Although clams can get out of hand, I have worked very well with clams and they stay in order. No shouting or carrying on if you know what I mean. They are adjusted. (After I manage them)

I am enclosing my resume for you.

I have supervised clams before and kept them in line; there's no trouble here. I make sure there's no problems with these clams. Under my supervision, clam trouble is kept to a minimum. They will not get out of hand. If there's an adjustment needed, I adjust. (If you know what I mean)

My resume is extensive. Please let me know when I start this job. Thank you. I look forward to hearing from you soon.

Sincerely,

Ted L. Nancy

P.S. I do not work with oysters; just clams

RESUME

TED L. NANCY

560 No. Moorpark Rd.
Apt #236
Thousand Oaks, CA 91360

1996-1997   Clam World   CLAMS MANAGER
                                       Contact: Doyle Fludge

Thank you for your interest in becoming a part of our innovative team at SCAN Health Plan. We are in receipt of your resumé, and we are reviewing it to determine if there is a match with our staffing needs at this time. If your background fits our needs, we will contact you within ten days of the postmark on this postcard.

For further information relating to current employment opportunities, please call our Job Hotline at (562) 989-5232. We wish you continued success in your employment search.

Sincerely,
Human Resources Department
EOE

You Go Uruguay I'll Go Mygway

We Both Go to Norgway

560 No. Moorpark Rd. Apt #236
Thousand Oaks, CA 91360   USA

Mar 9, 1998

Room Reservations
ARGENTINO HOTEL
Rambla de los
Argentinos s/n
Piriapolis, Uruguay

Dear Argentino Hotel:

I need a room for May 7, 1998. I have heard that your hotel
caters to those that need a room. I have a disease.

My disease has been acting up and has taken on a new level. I
blurt out Chinese waiter talk. In the middle of conversation I
yell out items taken off a Chinese menu. I can control it when I
write because I am not talking. But in public it is tough.

Just yesterday I was waiting to get a haircut - WE HAVE SWEET AND
SOUR MOO SHU AND PINEAPPLE CHUNKS FOR DESERT!! - at the barber
shop with my head in the shampoo sink when I noticed that the
barber - OUR LEMON CHICKEN IS IN A TANGY OYSTER SAUCE!!!! - chair
was ready to fall off its hinge. Had I not told the barber who
knows what may have happened. SNOW PEAS!

Please tell me if you have a room for May 7. A non smoking
room as - THAT COMES WITH YANG CHOW FRIED RICE!! - the cigarette
smoke makes me nauseous. Also, do you have a lap pool
because - WE ARE OUT OF SZECHUAN PEPPER BEEF. PLEASE TRY OUR KUNG
PAO COMBO!! - I like to swim.

Please let me know the rate for the room. Thank you. I have
heard that your hotel is the finest in Uruguay and that
you cater - NO SUBSTITUTIONS! - to travelers. The date again is
May 7.

Respectfully,

Ted L. Nancy

Ted L. Nancy

Hotel Casino Cabo Santa María - La Paloma
Gran Hotel Paysandú - Paysandú

Méndez Requena
HOTELES

ARGENTINO HOTEL CASINO PIRIAPOLIS
TURISMO DE SALUD

March 16, 1998

Mr. Ted L. Nancy
560 No. Moorpark Rd. Apt. 236
Thousand Oaks, CA 91360
U.S.A.

Dear Mr. Nancy:

Thank you for your letter dated March 9, 1998, in which you request a room reservation for May 7, 1998. We have made the reservation for one night.

I hereby attatch a brochure with the rates and accomodations that the Hotel has.

We would thank you if you could please let us know the length of your stay, and how you would be arriving.

You can contact us by fax at (598) 432 2791.

Sincerely,

Reneé Pereira de Méndez Requena
Director

Oficinas: Río Negro 1354 - Piso 5 - Esc. 31 - Tels.: 90 44 22 - 90 84 33 - Télex: TURISMR 23216 - Fax 90 22 37 - Montevideo - Uruguay
Buenos Aires - Santa Fé 834 - Tel/Fax: 3122114 - 3126412 - Bs. As. - Argentina

560 North Moorpark Rd.
Apt. #236
Thousand Oaks, CA 91360 USA

Feb 6, 1998

Customer Service Dept.
W. KOLTZOW FOODS
At Aker Brygge
Stranden 3
Oslo, Norway

Dear Customer Service:

I want to buy some Captain Stinks glove and bark polish. I have
used Captain Stinks for a long time and it really shines bark.
(And fish) Just rub it!

Also, do you have lox that can be sent to the USA as I have heard?

I have been told that W. Koltzow Fish Food Store helps EVERYONE
out there with their carp, trout, oysters, and glove stink polish.

Lets get this Captain Stinks product to my home and also the fish.
It's about time. My bark is dull! And I heard you have smoked
salmon in the shape of Robert DeNiro. (A true Norwegian.)   I
have Weejun shoes, but not Norwegian.

Thank you. I look forward to hearing from you soon. Where do I
send the check to? Tell me what fish you send to the USA. I want
it!

Respectfully,

Ted L. Nancy

Ted L. Nancy

Produktutvikling
Import - Eksport - Engros

Vareadresse : Kjøttbyen, Furuset, 1081 Oslo
Postadresse : Boks 33, Leirdal, 1008 Oslo
Sentralbord : 22 32 24 00
Telefax : 22 32 37 64
Bank : Chr. Bank og Kreditkasse
kto. 6554 05 02581
Postgiro : 0814 2253128
Foretaksreg. : NO 930206547 MVA

March 4 . 1998

Mr. Ted L.Nancy
560 North Moorpark Rd.
Apt. 236
Thousands Oaks
CA 91369
USA

Dear Sir

Thank you very much for your letter of Feb 6 . 1998.

We are flattered to learn that according what you have been told we help everyone-.
I am afraid some misunderstanding must have occurred..
We dont sell Captain Stinks glove and bark polish.
We dont export fish to USA.
We dont smoke salmon for mr. Niro.

So what is left then ?
Unfortunately nothing of what you were looking for.

We had great pleasure in reading your letter . and wish you all well !.

Best regards
W.Koltzow A/S

A.Ekse
man.dir.

Skalldyr Fisk Vilt Seafood Game Fruits de Mer Gibier Schalentiere Feinfisch Wild · Crostacei Pesce Cacciagione Mariscos Pescado Caza 海鮮魚 野味

560 No. Moorpark Rd. #236
Thousand Oaks, CA 91360

Aug 6, 1998

Room Reservations
HOTEL NORGE
Ole Bulls Pl. 4, 5012
Bergen, Norway

Dear Hotel Norge Reservations:

I will be arriving by sea shuttle Oct 1, 1998 and need a room for
3 nights Oct 1-3, 1998. I will make a mid air transfer to a sky
basket shifting over to a fuel pod halfway. I will then be
scuttled to an earth tote. (I have travel chits) Finally I will
land at your airport in a salt crate. I will then take a cab to
the Hotel Norge.

I have a special need when I arrive at your hotel:

I want to check in with my own tub. This is a standard size
bathtub that will hold 30 gallons of water. It is avocado green
in color so it should match MOST bathroom fixtures. I can carry
it up myself without disturbing other guests. I will go up the
side stairwell and make this in one trip. I have measured and it
will clear your desk area by 17 inches. Plenty of room! I can
maneuver it though the lobby with about 9 inches on each side. I
have a mirror attached to it so I can see what's to the left of
me.

It will take me about 4 hours to disconnect your tub and install
my tub. I have my own caulking gun and goo machine. I have done
this before with my own sink in Houston. Then I can completely
relax in my room.

Please tell me if you have a room for the 3 nights, Oct 1-3, and
how much is that room. Remember, I am using my own tub. I'll put
yours back the morning I checkout. Thank you. I look forward to
my info. You have been recommended.

Sincerely,

Ted L. Nancy

Ted L. Nancy

Ted L. Nancy
560 No. Moorpark Rd. #236
Thousand Oaks, CA 91360   Aug. 18, 1998
USA

Good afternoon Mr. Nancy.

Thank you very much for your letter. I am happy to offer you accommodation from
Oct. 1-3 at Radisson SAS Hotel Norge Bergen. The rate will be nok. 1715,- incl.
breakfast and taxes pr. night.

Regarding the bathtub I do appologize if we have given you the impression that it is
possible to bring one of your own. Unfortunately we cannot remove the bathtub
already installed in the room.

Please let me know if you would like me to make the reservation.

Again I thank you for your request and I am looking forward to hearing from you
again. I wish you the best of luck on your journey Mr. Nancy.

Best regards
Radisson SAS Hotel Norge Bergen

Tonje-Elisabeth Hansen
Reservations.

SAS Hotel Norge AS, Ole Bulls Plass 4, P.O. Box 662, N-5001 Bergen, Norway

Telephone: +47 55 57 30 00 Telefax: +47 55 57 30 01

Kreditkassen: 6501.05.76401 S.W.I.F.T. adress XIAN NO KK BGO
Reg. No. NO 976.611.942 MVA

Ted L. Nancy
560 No. Moorpark Rd. Apt #236
Thousand Oaks, Calif 91360 USA

MR. KNUT VOLLEBAEK
MINISTER OF FOREIGN AFFAIRS
7. Juni Plass 1,
Postbox 8114 Dep, N 0032
Oslo, Norway   Feb 7, 1998

Dear Honorable Mr. Knut,

A relative of mine just finished working on the U.S. Army's camel
experiment. There was a cow and a camel at my home. I think the
camel got the cow pregnant. They must think they are still in
Bhazazzadan. The cows tongue feels like plush velour. It would
make a great sock.

The cow has not been with anything. (Except 1 night when the
camel got out). Do you think there are burgers here? Would
people eat half camel, half cow? What would that look like?

Because of my deep respect for Norway I want to give this "camow"
to you. (Some call it a "cowmel") I have many memories of your
great country and your incredible people and feel this camel-cow
would be symbolic of those feelings. Perhaps you can put it on
your new flag. You have the best fjords!

This animal should be able to store up to 20 gallons of milk in
its hump. Can pull on teats for three days without rest.

Please accept this gift. Who should I ship it to? Will be
arriving by barge in April. I look forward to your reply. Norway
is the best country and you are the best leader. I admire that
you accept gifts from U.S. people.

With Great Admiration,

Ted L. Nancy

Ted L. Nancy

Royal Ministry of Foreign Affairs
The Minister of Foreign Affairs

Mr. Ted L. Nancy
560 No. Moorpark Rd. Apt #236
Thousand Oaks, Calif 91360 USA

3/ March,1998

Dear Mr. Nancy,

I read your letter concerning the "camow", with great interest. It seems to me that the miracle that contributed to the creation of this new creature, is not only on a par with the creation of "Dolly", but by far surpasses it. "Dolly" will probably be copied many times in the future. I doubt, however, although I may be wrong, that we will ever again experience anything close to the "camow". For this reason I would suggest that the "camow" remain with you. However, I would love to come and inspect it on my next trip to the US.

Clearly the "camow" could revolutionise agriculture in Norway, so I have passed the letter on to my colleague the Minister of Agriculture for more detailed consideration.

With great respect

Knut Vollebæk

c.c. Minister of Agriculture, Mr. Kåre Gjønnes

Postal Address:	Office Address:	Telephone:	Telex:	Telefax:	Cable:
P.O. Box 8114 DEP. N-0032 Oslo Norway	7. juni plassen/ Victoria Terrasse 0251 Oslo	(47) 22 24 36 00	71004 NOREG N	(47) 22 83 39 34	NOREG, Oslo

560 No. Moorpark Rd. Apt #236
Thousand Oaks, CA 91360 USA

Feb 9, 1998

Reservations
PLAZA FUERTE HOTEL
Bartolome Mitre 1361
Montevideo, Uruguay

Dear Plaza Fuerte Hotel:

I have recently had all my teeth removed and replaced with lobster
meat. I feel this is the best thing for me. My teeth are not as
hard as before but they certainly can chew, although not as good.
I can eat most foods. (Not cookies). I don't worry about
bacteria. My lobster teeth are secured on good.

Now to my question: Do you have a room for 3 nights April 22-24,
1998? I need 4 double beds in the room. But I will be traveling
by myself. (My wife left me).

I would also like to know what kind of restaurant you have in your
hotel. You are highly recommended by a man who had his teeth
removed and replaced with sausage links. That's why I am writing
you. I have heard that your hotel is probably the finest in all
of Uruguay and that many travelers stay there so I will feel at
home. He told me he did.

Please tell what's available. Also, do you still give out
Bavarian Funbags at checkout? The particulars again: Apr 22-24,
lobster meat for teeth, 4 double beds. Thank you. I look forward
to a speedy reply from the finest hotel in Uruguay.

Sincerely,

Ted L. Nancy
Ted L. Nancy

PLAZA FUERTE HOTEL

18th Feb, 1998.

Dear Mr. L. Nancy:

It was a great pleasure to receive your letter. It was the funniest reservation someone has ever sent to us.

In reply to your questions:
1 - We do have a double room for 3 nights (from April 22nd to 25th)
2 - It only has one double bed, or a double bed and a single one in the same room.
3 - We have an international restaurant and a very nice pub, where you can have drinks and simple dishes

Our rates are: MINISUITE SINGLE — US$ 165
      SUITE   — US$ 300

These rates include breakfast and taxes. You can have a 15% discount if you make your reservation through a company.

Please, in case of confirming the reservation, we need a credit card number with exp. date and security code (if it is a Master Card).

Could you please send a fax with the confirmation as soon as possible?

Best regards,

Lucia Pereira

(LUCIA PEREIRA)
RECEPTION.

560 No. Moorpark Rd. Apt #236
Thousand Oaks, CA 91360   USA

Apr 2, 1999

Room Reservations
PLAZA FUERTE HOTEL
Bartolome Mitre 1361
Montevideo, Uruguay

Dear Plaza Fuerte Hotel:

In my last letter, if you remember, I needed a room at your fine
hotel for 3 nights Apr 22-24, 1998, and I was having my teeth
replaced with lobster meat. You were kind enough to write me
back.

I now must change that reservation. I am now arriving in Uruguay
May 15, 1999 for 3 days. And, in addition to having my teeth
replaced with lobster meat, I am also having my toenails removed
and replaced with ham slices. While my toenails won't be as hard
as before, the ham will certainly keep dirt out.

I will wear open toe sandals so you will be able to see ham slices
where my toenails used to be. (There is no stink here!)

I have heard your hotel is the finest in all of Uruguay.

Can you tell me how I reserve a room for these dates? Again, May
15, 16, 17, 1999. What do I do? Thank you.

Also do you still give out Poppyseed Squints at checkout? I look
forward to hearing from you soon with info. You are very
accommodating. I have heard you welcome those with lobster teeth
and ham slice toenails.

Sincerely,

Ted L. Nancy
Ted L. Nancy

To: Mr Ted L Nancy
    560 N. Moorpark Rd.
    #236
    Thousand Oaks, CA 91360
    USA

Bartolome ~~Mitre~~ 1363/3750
MONTEV

560 No. Moorpark Rd. Apt #236
Thousand Oaks, CA 91360 USA

Apr 15, 1998

Room Reservations
AMBASSADEUR HOTEL
Camilla Colletts vei 15, 0258
Oslo, Norway

Dear Room Reservations:

I need a room for three nights June 1-3, 1998.

I will practice applauding in the room. I will start off with a
light, warm smattering of applause and I will build up to loud
vigorous clapping. (I may throw a few bravos in)

I will practice this applauding every day from 7 in the morning
until noon, order my meal in, then start applauding again at 1:00
o'clock. I go until 6 in the evening. At times it will be a
thunderous applause and I may jump up but mostly it will be a
steady applauding. (I may throw a few 'mores' in.)   There will
be some raves and a few cheers, but let me be candid with you -
this is STRICTLY applauding. (I may pound my knee)

This is important so that when I am called on to applaud at the
show later on I will get it right. In my country (USA) applauding
is a sign of a job well done.

My question: Do you have pineapple in your coleslaw?

I look forward to my stay at your hotel. I have heard that the
Ambassadeur Hotel is the finest in Norway and that applauders are
treated with the highest courtesy. Please tell me if you have a
room available for June 1-3. Thank you. I look forward to
hearing from you soon.

Sincerely,

Ted L. Nancy

Ted L. Nancy

Ted L. Nancy
560 No. Moorpark Rd.#236

·US -91360   THOUSANDS OAKS, CA.

Hotel Ambassadeur Best Western
Camilla Colletts vei 15
N-0258 OSLO
Telefon 22 44 18 35
Telefax 22 44 47 91
Postgiro: 0824 0590027
Bankgiro: 2070.05.04655
NO 950 181 478 MVA

D.   27.04.1998

We thank you for yor letter of April 15, and are sorry
to inform you that we are fully booked in the wanted
period from June 1 - 3, 1998.

Best regards
HOTEL AMBASSADEUR BEST WESTERN

Gretha·Wiik Nilsen

560 No. Moorpark Rd. Apt #236
Thousand Oaks, CA 91360   USA

Room Reservations
GRAND HOTEL
Karl Johans GT. 31, 0159
Oslo, Norway   Aug 26, 1998

Dear Grand Hotel

Hello. I recently heard of your hotel through The Bib Barn where
they advertise it. I need a room for 2 nights: Oct 17-18, 1998.
Your finest suite, please.

I am a 55 year old white male, 5'6" 240 pounds, boils. I sound
just like Carol Channing. I will sit in your lobby for hours and
talk like Carol Channing. And don't worry I sound just like her.
"Charles never touched me in 48 years of marriage." I wear a
blond wig and big red lipstick. "Why if it isn't Dolly Levi, the
irreplaceable matchmaker."

Others in your lobby will remark that man sounds just like Carol
Channing. While others will say I wish he would shut up. You
must take the good with the bad. "Who likes squish noises? I
don't like squish noises. Diamonds are a girl's best friend."

Also, do you have laundry facilities in the lobby so I can wash
out my sport bra when needed?

Please tell me what the room rate is for those 2 nights - Oct 17-
18. I am in need of this information soon as I must make travel
plans NOW.

Your hotel is HIGHLY REGARDED by those in the know. I have a tank
of anchovies I take with me.

Thank you for writing me with info.

Sincerely,

Ted L. Nancy

GRAND
HOTEL
ET RICA HOTEL

Ted L. Nancy
560 No. Moorpark Rd. Apt. 236
Thousand Oaks, CA 91360
USA

Oslo 7th September 1998

Dear Ted L. Nancy,

Thank you for your kind letter regarding a room reservation at our hotel. We are very sorry to inform that we are fully booked during the periode of the requested dates.

With kind regards
Grand Hotel

Bente C. Svendsen
Sales Manager

560 No. Moorpark Rd. #236
Thousand Oaks, CA 91360   USA

Feb 8, 1998

Reservations
ALCAZAR HOTEL
Avda. Piria 901
Piriapolis, Uruguay

Dear Alcazar Hotel,

I would like a room for 5 nights, Apr 19-23, 1998.

I will check in with 1000 butter pats. I will then turn the heat
up in the room to over 110 degrees. I will stay in the room for
the full 5 days with these butter pats.

When I leave the room on the morning of the 24th, I will have
spent 120 hours alone in my room in the heat with 1000 pats of
butter.

Do you have a room available for Apr 19-23? I will bring my own
butter pats. I will clean up all butter mess on the morning of
the 24th. There will be NO butter left in the room. No stains
will be left on the chairs or carpet from the melted butter.

I have done this before with tarter sauce and DID NOT leave any
droppings. (All smell was aired in 2 hours). Please let me know
if a room is available for the dates I need? I look forward to a
prompt reply from you as I have to make my business travel plans
very soon. Thank you.

Sincerely,

Ted L. Nancy
Ted L. Nancy

Piriápolis 11 de Abril de 1998.

Señor Ted L. Nancy

Presente.

De mi mayor consideración:

Acuso recibo de su anterior carta de reservación.Pido disculpa por no contestar enseguida.Disponemos de la comodidad que Ud. desea del 19 al 23 de Mayo de 1998.La terifa diaria con desayuno para la fecha es de Treinta Dólares (U$S 30.).Deseamos saber si la manteca que Ud trae tiene marca registrada en el Uruguay y si tiene mercado co mercializable,siendo de su cargo la entrada de alimentos al pais.Si decide su estadia rogamos girar una seña del Veinte por ciento (20%) por el Western Union Cambio Gales Montevideo a la orden del Hotel Alcazar.

Esperando su respuesta lo sa luda atentamente:

Por Hotel Alcazar:

ANABEL DE LEON ARAUJO.

DEMENTED

560 No. Moorpark Road
Apt #236
Thousand Oaks, CA 91360

Feb 10, 1997

Customer Satisfaction Dept.
Hospeco
HEALTH GUARDS TOILET SEAT COVERS
7501 Carnegie Ave.
Cleveland, OH 44103

Dear Health Guards Toilet Seat Covers:

I feel you have the best toilet seat guard out there. I have used many. Yours are the best. Yesterday, I was telling a stranger on the bus about your toilet seat guards and she agreed. She said I knew what I was talking about. Then she went back to her book. What other fabrics do they come in beside tissue paper? I have heard of straw. Why?

I once used one of your toilet seat covers for a cowboy hat. It fit perfectly. You punch through the hole as normal and the top pops up and you put it on your head like a cowboy hat. Your ready to line dance!

Can I buy traveling toilet seat covers directly from you? I WILL NOT sit down unless I have a Health Guard Toilet Seat Protector under me. That is my rule. I'm thinking of moving to Rangoon. What do you think? Are your seat covers there? I have heard of those filthy Rangoon toilet seats.

Thanks for making the BEST out there. I tell anyone who sits on a toilet seat. Some listen. I have been slapped. Send me literature on the newest toilet cover models.

Sincerely,

Ted L. Nancy

Ted L. Nancy

Hospital Specialty Company

Personal Care Division of the Tranzonic Companies

7501 Carnegie Avenue • Cleveland, Ohio 44103-4896

P.O. Box 94763 • Cleveland, Ohio 44101-4763

(800) 321-9832 • (216) 361-1230 • (800) B-AT-EASE

FAX (216) 361-0829

February 27, 1997

Ted L. Nancy
560 No. Moorpark Road
Apt. #236
Thousand Oaks, CA   91360

    Just a note to say "Thank you". Hospital Specialty is very proud of the products we manufacture and we are appreciative of any feed back we get from the users. Enclosed please find samples for your use.

    Thanks again.

Regards,

Kathy Metzger
Vice President Administration

enclosure

Ted L. Nancy
560 No. Moorpark Rd.   #236
Thousand Oaks, CA 91360

PRESIDENT CLINTON
The White House
1600 Pennsylvania Avenue
Washington, D.C. 20500   Feb 1, 1996

Dear President Clinton,

I think you are a great president and are doing a great job for
our country. I will vote for you all the way. I know that you
sometimes send a note of congratulations to senior citizens who
have reached their 100th birthday. That is just great! These
folks really appreciate that. Let me tell you, I know. Anybody
reaching their 100th birthday and getting a greeting from the
President of the United States must be feeling pretty good.

The reason I am writing is I want to tell you about my 100 year
old turtle. His name is also Socks. And he's been in our family
for almost 100 years. Socks' birthday is Feb 4th, 1996. We have
been caring for this segenetarion turtle since his birth. He was
brought over on a ship and has been in our family living on a
plantation, then a farm, and for a long time at a zoo. Now he is
living in my garage.

I was wondering if a birthday greeting can also be sent to this
octonagarian turtle that's been passed on in my family for
generation after generation? He loves our president. And if he
were not a turtle he would vote for you. So forget that Socks is
a turtle and just think it's another voter when you send the
greeting.

Bless you, Sir, for being a great leader and a friend to all. I
hope my turtle can get a birthday greeting from you. If not,
maybe just a picture of you. I will show it to him.

Respectfully,

Ted L. Nancy
& Socks

Best Wishes,   Bill Clinton

560 No. Moorpark Rd. Apt #236
Thousand Oaks, CA 91360   USA

May 5, 1999

Room Reservations
HOTEL AGRA ASHOK, IDTC
6-B Mall Rd.
Agra - 282 001, India

Dear Hotel Agra Ashok:

I have been recommended by pebble venders to your 27 star hotel.
I need a room for 1 week starting Jul 21st, 1999. I will be
arriving by turtle.

I have a problem which I like to address while visiting a new
hotel. I eat the drapes. I munch on the blinds. I chew the
cord. I once stuffed a whole curtain into my mouth then spent 10
minutes at a broken soda machine. Never again! Do you have a
knit drape? Those are the easiest to digest. Take a credit card
imprint from me. I want to be charged. Let's you and I come up
with a fair price for my room and for me eating your drapes. I
will NOT eat velour canopies!

I have heard you go out of your way for those that eat their
drapes. How much? Will you squeeze my bump?

Please answer quickly as I am traveling and need to secure
reservations now and also I want to be able to digest the drapes.
Thank you.

Sincerely,

Ted L. Nancy

I am getting sleepy now. But I must continue to write my letters. I feel
the medicine under my tongue more then usual. It tastes like parakeet seeds.
My ankles are swollen up like tetherballs. Sometimes I itch. Hey! I smelled a
tuna belch this morning on my neighbor's breath when he asked me to
move my car. I'm sure it was tuna and I'm sure it was my neighbor. I'm not so
sure it was my car...

560 No. Moorpark Rd. Apt #236
Thousand Oaks, CA. 91360   USA

Reservations
Hotel Agra Ashok, IDTC
6-B Mall Rd.
Agra - 282 001, India

Dear Hotel Agra Ashok,

I recently wrote to you about room reservations and I have not
heard back.

Can you tell me if you have a room for 7 days? My trip has been
changed from Jul 21st until Oct 1st. I would like to make my
reservations now.   Your finest accomodations please.

Please tell me how much a superior room is for 1 week.

I look forward to hearing from you soon.

You have been highly recommended. Others have told me of your
fine hotel and I look forward to a relaxing stay. Can you also
tell me if you have a concierge that can assist me?   Thank you.

Sincerely,

Ted L. Nancy

होटल आगरा अशोक
Hotel Agra Ashok

6 B Mall Road Agra- 282001 Uttar Pradesh
Tel 76223-27, 73271-74
Cables ASHOKOTEL Telex 0565-313 HAA IN

The
Ashok
Group

26th July,1999

To,
Ms Ted L. Nancy,
560 No., Moorpart Road
Apartment # 236,
Thousand Oaks,
CA. 91360 USA.

Dear Madam,

Please refer your letter regarding booking of 01 Room for 07 days at our Hotel.

Our Room RATES are as under :

Sgl	:	Rs.1500.00
Double	:	Rs.2500.00
Suite	:	Rs.3000.00

Taxes 5% extra.

You have not mentioned whether you will be staying Single/Double. However, please note that your booking is Confirmed and rest all your requirment can be taken care of when you Check into our Hotel. Also please let us know whether you require any transport facility ?

Awaiting your arrival at our Hotel.

Thanking you for showing interest in our Hotel.

Yours sincerely

(SANJEEV KUMAR DASS)
Manager (FO)

रजिस्टर्ड कार्यालय : भारत पर्यटन विकास निगम लि. जीवन विहार 3 संसद मार्ग नई दिल्ली 110001 फोन 310923. 310597 तार पर्यटन टेलेक्स 031-63361
Regd. Office: India Tourism Development Corporation Ltd. Jeevan Vihar 3 Sansad Marg New Delhi 110001 Tel 310923. 310597 Cables TOURISM Telex 031-83361

560 No. Moorpark Rd. #236
Thousand Oaks, Ca. 91360

3/17/99

PARTYLITE
59 Armstrong Rd.
Plymouth, Ma. 02360

Dear Partylite Candle Company,

I just received some of your Tropical Blossom low temperature
candles. I was told that to prevent fires, the flame burns at
just 100 degrees. Finally, I can get drapes. I was vacationing
in Palm Springs and it was 120 degrees outside. Does that mean I
could step into a giant candle flame of yours and be cooled off?
You should sell it as "the flame that refreshes."

What happens if it gets to be 103 degrees in my house? Will the
PARTYLITE candles burst on? Should I put them in the refrigerator
when it gets that hot?

Also, how much would it cost to have a candle made big enough to
stand in, to impress my neighbors? I can handle a hundred degrees
easy. My jacuzzi is hotter than that.

I am looking forward to all your answers.

Sincerely,

Ted L. Nancy
Ted L. Nancy

PARTYLITE®

P.O. BOX 976

PLYMOUTH

MASSACHUSETTS

0 2 3 6 2

508•830•3100

FAX 508•830•1488

April 28, 1999

Mr. Ted L. Nancy
560 N. Moorpark Rd., #236
Thousand Oaks, CA 91360

Dear Mr. Nancy:

Thank you for your recent letter to PartyLite Gifts, Inc., and for your fascinating questions about our candles. We appreciate your interest in our products, and we are happy to address the "hot" topics you brought up!

A candle that burns at just 100 degrees would be a cool candle indeed - our candles are very cool, but not that cool. While they do tend to burn cooler than most, the average temperature for our molten wax is 126 degrees Fahrenheit. The flame melting the wax ranges anywhere from 400 degrees to 550 degrees Fahrenheit. Although your idea was a good one, we don't think these statistics would stand behind the slogan "the flame that refreshes."

We can certainly understand your excitement over the prospect of finally getting new drapes. Our feeling is that a window without drapes is like a candle without a flame - it's just not complete. Please be aware, however, that yes, our candles do burn cooler than most, but the flame can still ignite drapery and other flammable objects. To avoid such an incident, be sure to keep all such items at least one foot from the burning candle.

You needn't worry about PartyLite candles spontaneously combusting under any circumstances. There just isn't any way our candles can self-ignite. Our goal is to add beauty and delight to our customers' lives, and to try not to bring them unwanted surprises at inopportune moments.

Believe it or not, yours is the first request we've ever received for a life-sized, walk-in candle. It's a unique idea to be sure. And there's little doubt your neighbors would be impressed. But owning such a candle and using it, as you suggest, to replace your Jacuzzi would not only be dangerous and fatuous, but it would put you, as we say in the candle business, in deep wax.

Again, Mr. Nancy, thank you for your interest in PartyLite products. We appreciate your enthusiasm, and hope to do business with you soon!

Sincerely,

Cheryl A. Hoitt
Correspondence Department

560 No. Moorpark Rd. #236
Thousand Oaks, CA 91360 USA

Jan 5, 2000

Reservations
RELAIS DUE LAGHI HOTEL
loc. la cerque 00061
Anguillara,
Sebazia (RM) Italy

Dear Relais Due Laghi Hotel:

I wish to stay at your 41 star hotel for 6 nights Feb 15-20, 2000.
Your finest room with twin beds, please. I am a trampoline
demonstrator touring Italy.

While in my room I will play whale sounds on my tape recorder.
These can get loud especially when I turn it up to 7. These are
sounds of whales enjoying themselves; blow hole sounds and some
brushing against each other. There will be mating and whale
sadness. Will this disturb the other guests? This will be for 6
days.

The whale noise is loud and can drift down the hall. If I'm in
room 42 and you go down to room 58 that should be quiet around
there. I just want to be honest with you regarding these whale
sounds.

I look forward to an answer from you if you do have a room for my
stay. I have heard that your hotel accepts whale noises coming
from the room at night. Also, do you give out party peeps at
checkout? Thank you very much. I have heard great things about
the Relais Due Laghi Hotel in Italy. One returning guest said she
had a sea shnitzel sandwich there that was out of this world. I
want it.

Sincerely,

Ted L. Nancy

★ ★ ★ ★

Relais I due Laghi
Localita' Le Cerque
00061 Anguillara Sabazia
ROMA – ITALY

Anguillara S., 11 gennaio 2000

Dear Miss Ted,

many thanks for your kind and........honest letter!

We love very much everythung concerning the animals we have in the 400 acres estate:
horses, cows, goats, sheep. So you could menage whale sounds not into the Relais but
outside in the farm.

In fact our Guests come in our Relais because of the silence we guaranteee to them.

We send to you our depliant and price list.

With best regards we remain.

Front-office
Cristina Ciociola

e mail duelaghi@edl it   www venere it/lazio/due_laghi
I Due Laghi Country Relais · Località Le Cerque · 00061 Anguillara Sabazia (Roma) · Tel. 06 99607059 r.a. · Fax 06 99607068

560 No. Moorpark Rd. Apt #236
Thousand Oaks, CA 91360

Mar 3, 1998

Smokers Service Dept.
NICODERM PATCH
C/O SmithKline Beecham
780 5th Ave.
King Of Prussia, PA 19406-1437

Dear Nicoderm Patch Co.:

I am trying to quit smoking. I know you make the Nicoderm Patch.
Now I am looking for the Nicoderm Blanket which I believe you
make. This is for when the patch doesn't work. This is a blanket
that I put over me and walk around ingesting nicotine into me.
This blanket covers my whole body as I walk through the city
learning how to stop smoking.

I would also like to special order another Nicoderm Jumpsuit. I
ingest phenopolapopaleen into me. Should I send a check for
$2,357.42 like before? Has the price changed? Is Howie still
there?

Please write soon as I think my jumpsuit is out of nicotine.
Thank you very much.

Sincerely,

Ted L. Nancy

Ted L. Nancy

Trying To Quit

SmithKline Beecham
Consumer Healthcare

August 4, 1998

Mr. Ted L. Nancy
560 North Moorpark Road
Apt. 236
Thousand Oaks, CA 91360

Dear Mr. Nancy:

Thank you for contacting us.

At SmithKline Beecham Consumer Healthcare, we market the Nicoderm CQ patch and Nicorette gum as our stop smoking aids. We do not market any other smoking cessation aids. Enclosed is information about Nicoderm CQ and Nicorette as well as information about some of our other products.

Your interest in our products is appreciated.

Sincerely yours,

Julie Sheppard

Julie Sheppard
Product Information Specialist

725113953

PO Box 1467, Pittsburgh, PA 15230. Telephone (412) 928 1000.

560 No. Moorpark Rd.
Suite #236
Thousand Oaks, CA 91360

Advertising Dept.
DALLAS MORNING NEWS
5801 Marvin D. Love Fwy #20
Dallas, TX 75237   Sep 2, 1998

Dear Dallas Morning News:

I have a business that I want to advertise in your newspaper.
Please tell me how much to run an ad in your paper? A quarter
page will be fine. Thank you. Here is my ad:

**Can't meet anyone? Never had a date? Died and still
haven't met anyone? Never be alone again. Even in death.
Meet the partner of your choice when you get fixed up by
Cre-Mates.**

**Here's how it works. You die, we cremate you, we take
your ashes to our dating room. We show your urn pictures
of others that we think may interest you. These are also
people that passed on. And had the same interests as you.
We cremate them and then we put your ashes and their ashes
together in one urn and sprinkle the whole thing on top of
whoever you say to. That triples your chances of meeting
someone!**

**Why stop dating just because you're dead? With Cre-Mates
we can fix you up. Scatter yourself with the perfect
mate. One call and one cremation does it all. (My
address here)**

Please let me know how much to run my ad. If you have a dating
section that might be the best place for it. If not, tell me what
sections you have. I look forward to getting information from you
for my ad. Thank you.

Sincerely,

Ted L. Nancy
President Cre-Mates Dating Service

The Dallas Morning News

Dear Advertiser:

We acknowledge and thank you for your advertisement to be published in The Dallas Morning News. However, at this time, we choose not to publish this advertisment.

Thank you for your concern and cooperation in this matter.

Sincerely,
THE DALLAS MORNING NEWS

Irma Houchen

Classified Advertising Supervisor
Classified Advertising Department

Communications Center, P.O. Box 655237, Dallas. Texas 75265, 214/977-8222

560 No. Moorpark Rd. #236
Thousand Oaks, CA 91360

Classifieds Information
WORCESTER TELEGRAM & GAZETTE NEWSPAPER
713 Main St.
Fitchburg, MA 01420   Sep 7, 1999

Dear Worcester Telegram & Gazette Newspaper,

I am interested in rate information for your newspaper. I have
many readers in the Massachusetts area. My self published books
are well received. I now want to place an ad in your newspaper to
sell my latest books. Here is my ad:.

I am the sole author of the bestselling German book "Toby The
Urinating Mule". This is a very funny book about a mule with
prostate problems and he has to urinate a lot. Great fun for
everyone especially those with prostate problems. You should see
where Toby goes? His escapades with Woody Harrelson's picture are
hilarious. Now ready for publication. I am accepting offers up
until 3 o'clock Today. Do not even attempt to make an offer past
3 o'clock. Like the car parking sign says: Don't even think
about it.

I also have the bestselling books: "Blimpi The Lopsided Slug"
which is a Parisian pop-up book. And I wrote "Lumpy The Nicotine
Addicted Goat". Publication offers for those books will be until
2 o'clock Tomorrow and like the car parking sign says: If You
Even Think About It - DON'T!

How much is it to run my ad in your classifieds section?

Thank you. I look forward to hearing from you soon with rate
information. The Worcester Telegram is a fine newspaper. I read
it here alot after I get it out of the bin.

Sincerely,

Ted L. Nancy
German Author

Sept. 10, 1999

Ted L. Nancy
560 No. Moorpark Rd. #236
Thousand Oaks, CA.91360

Dear Mr. Nancy,

Thank you for your interest in the Telegram & Gazette.

We are the only daily newspaper in Worcester. We publish
7 days a week and our rates are very competitive.

You can place your advertising message in our newspaper
from 1 day to 1 year! Your advertising message will reach
over 350,000 readers on 1 Sunday alone.

Enclosed you will find 2 rate sheets; one for the Adult
Classification rates, the other for Mail Order rates.
It is the Telegram & Gazette policy to have on hand a
copy of your books.

We accept Mastercard, Visa and Discover and you may
call us anytime Mon. thru Thur. 8-5 and Fri. 8-7.
For your convenience our out-of-state toll free number is
1-800-678-6680.

If you have any questions please contact me and again thank
you for your inquiry into Classified Advertising in the
Telegram & Gazette. We look forward to serving all of your
advertising needs.

Sincerely,

Giovanna Morrissey,
Telemarketing Supervisor
(508)-793-9362

560 No. Moorpark Rd. Suite #236
Thousand Oaks, CA 91360

Carpet Sales Dept.
A & B CARPETS/FLOOR COVERINGS
14709 S. Western Ave.
Gardenia, CA 90249   Apr 23, 1999

Dear A & B Carpets:

I will be opening 6 of my stores in the Gardenia area very soon. I
will need to carpet all my stores and I was referred to you.

I own SLIVERS N' SHARDS. We carry all slivers and most shards.
We are not associated with the "Shards and Slivers Superstore."
That's not us. The carpeting should be silver.

We sell hotel soap slivers by the bag. We have them all including
hard to find Zest. Cut off a shard to fit your needs. Visit our
splinter section. We believe splinters are really small shards
but are medium sized slivers. Buy your next splinter from us and
we throw in a sliver. That's 1 sliver, 1 shard, and 2 splinters
all for the price of a sliver. All our salesmen have freckles.
We offer a money back guarantee on all shards. Bring it back if
you are not happy. Sorry, slivers are not refundable. We carry
the 2 foot shard. Take one home today.

Remember, if it's a sliver, a shard, or even a splinter (but not a
chunk) it's probably from Slivers N' Shards (unless it's from THE
SHARD SHACK OR THE SLIVERS AND SHARDS SUPERSTORE.)

Please contact me with carpeting information so I may get an
estimate. I have heard that A & B Carpets is the finest at
customer service and has the best prices. Should I just buy the
carpet from you and install it myself or can you install it for me
in all 6 stores? Thank you. I await your reply.

Sincerely,

Ted L. Nancy

Mr. Ted L. Nancy

A&B
Quality
FLOOR COVERING
CARPET • VINYL • HARDWOOD • TILE

4-27-99

Dear Mr. Nancy,

Thank-you for your inquiry concerning carpet for your 6 new stores in Gardenia. Regretfully we have just signed a multi-year contract with Simmons International Shards & Slivers. As you can imagine this will consume much of our time for the next several years. Good Luck with the opening of your 6 new stores.

Sincerely,

A & B

14709 S. WESTERN AVENUE • GARDENA, CA 90249 • (310) 532-7113 • 532-0753
Contractor's License #381217

560 No. Moorpark Rd.   Apt #236
Thousand Oaks, CA 91360 USA

Apr 26, 1999

Reservations
CLARKS SHIRAZ HOTEL
54 Taj Rd,
Agra - 282 001, India

Dear Clarks Shiraz Hotel:

I will be arriving by muleback 16 July, 1999. I need a room for
16 Jul through 27 Jul, 1999. A millennium room please as I look
directly into the sun.

Because of my tender feet I wear bananas for shoes. I attach 2
bananas under each foot and walk on these. Please have the maid
NOT take my bananas at night. They are my shoes.

I heard you were receptive to banana shoe wearing guests. Will
you tug my hem?

Please tell me if you have a room for 10 days, 16 Jul on? I am
addicted to 2nd hand smoke. Can you put me next to someone who
smokes so I can inhale their cigarette smell? Also, after I eat I
need to smell smoke. Please seat me in the dining room properly.
Thank you.

I have heard wonderful things of your hotel. Some good.

Thank you. I await my reply.

Sincerely,

Ted L. Nancy

HOTEL

Clarks Shiraz

54, Taj Road, Agra -282 001 India

Tel. :361421-7 Fax : 0562-361428 Telex : 0565-211 Grams : SHIRAZ

CLARKS
GROUP OF
HOTELS

To   3rd May,1999
Ms.Ted L.Nancy
560 No.Moorpark Rd. Apt #236
Thousand Oaks,
CA 91360 USA.

Dear Madam,

We are in receipt of your letter dated 26th April,1999 with
full of fun and fury.

Though,you are not expecting any reply to your letter, still
it is our bounden duty to acknowledge the receipt of the same.

We have noted the contents of your letter and shall try to comply
with your request.

As desired by you, we are pleased to confirm a single occupancy
room for your stay from 16th To 27th July,1999 @US$ 45/- (U S
Dollar Forty Five Only) per night on room only basis plus 5%
Government Tax.

If acceptable, please send a line of your confirmation alongwith
a minimum 50% as an advance deposit of the room charges latest by
1st June,1999 which will enable us to hold the accommodation on
definite basis.

Looking forward to hearing from you soon.

Thanking you and with kind regards.

Yours sincerely,
for Hotel Clarks Shiraz.

(Ram Adhar Yadav)
Asstt.Manager-Reservation

P/*

Regd. Off. : U.P. HOTELS LTD., 1101-1102, "Surya Kiran" Building, 19, Kasturba Gandhi Marg, New Delhi-110001

HOTEL	HOTEL	HOTEL	HOTEL	HOTEL
CLARKS SHIRAZ	CLARKS AMER	CLARKS VARANASI	CLARKS AVADH	CLARKS BUNDELA
AGRA	JAIPUR	VARANASI	LUCKNOW	KHAJURAHO

560 No. Moorpark Rd. #236
Thousand Oaks, CA 91360 USA

GUINNESS BOOK OF RECORDS
Guinness Publishing Ltd.
33 London Road
Enfield
EN2 6DJ
England   Feb 17, 1997

Dear Guinness Book Of Records:

Is this a record? Yesterday I went to 4 different stores and
purchased items. Do you believe at all 4 stores I HAD EXACT
CHANGE EACH TIME!

TO DOCUMENT:

Place One. I bought a spatula and a mallet. $3.21. I had three
one dollar bills, two dimes and a penny.

Place Two. I bought yellow striped shorty pajamas. $19.67. I
had a ten, a five, four ones, and two quarters and 17 pennies.

Place Three. I bought an alligator clock, shampoo, and a hamster.
$222.99. I had two one hundred dollar bills, a twenty, two ones,
3 quarters, 2 dimes, and four pennies.

Place Four. I bought another spatula, a spark plug, a Boxcar
Willie cassette (used), a mitten, and some guava jam. $59.12. I
had a fifty, nine ones, a dime, and two pennies.

All these places can be documented by receipts and picture of me
in my pajamas with my clock and spatulas holding my Boxcar Willie
cassette (which I have since returned) and petting my hamster.

Please let me know if I am in receipt of a world record and what I
can expect in the way of rewards. Please send me the guidelines
for this event. Thank you very much.

Sincerely,

Ted L. Nancy
Ted L. Nancy

GUINNESS PUBLISHING

Mr T L Nancy
560 No. Moorpark Road #236
Thousand Oaks
CA 91360
USA

27 March, 1997

Dear Mr Nancy

Thank you for your enquiry of 17 February 1997 when you advised that you went to four different stores and purchased items and had the exact change each time.

We have examined your proposal in detail, but we are afraid that we have to inform you that what you propose is not currently suitable for publication in The Guinness Book of Records. We receive over 10,000 enquiries a year, and only a very small proportion are used to establish new categories.

We are sorry that we cannot be more positive but we thank you again for your enquiry and your interest in The Guinness Book of Records.

Yours sincerely

Amanda Brooks
Correspondence Editor

338 Euston Road · London NW1 3BD · Telephone: +44 (0) 171 891 4567 · Fax: +44 (0) 171 891 4501 · Email: Guinness_Publishing@guinness.com

Registered in England, Company Number 541295 · Registered Office: 39 Portman Square · London W1H 0EE
Guinness Publishing is a business name of Guinness Publishing Limited.

560 No Moorpark Rd. #236
Thousand Oaks, CA 91360

Apr 23, 1999

Merchant Help Line
CHAMBER OF COMMERCE ZANESVILLE
205 N. 5th St.
Zanesville, OH 43701

Dear Chamber Of Commerce:

It has been proven that a good mall needs an exhibit from time to
time to attract shoppers.

I am interested in having a showing of my photographs in your
malls. My exhibit is called: "PICTURES OF ROBERT DUVALL'S BACK."
This is a group of photographs of Robert Duvall's back. (I think
it's him. A person came up to me and I took the pictures. He
said it was him.)

This will bring the shoppers in like wildfire. Attract people
exclusively to the Zanesville malls. It has been proven that my
exhibit attracts shoppers. In France there were near stampedes to
get close to the pictures. Do you want to see them? I can send
you a sample of these photos of the great actor's back if you'd
like to see them. (I hope it was him. He said it was and then we
both went and watched "The Apostle" together at the Cineplex 17).

I will need security. Can you supply this? What is the cost?

Please let me know how I arrange this showing at your malls and if
you would like to see these pictures. They are very European.
You can see the back puffed out. Even one where he has his hand
up. Thank you. I look forward to hearing from you soon. Can you
please send me a list of Zanesville malls I can write to? Thank
you.

Sincerely,

Ted L. Nancy

Zanesville-Muskingum County Chamber of Commerce

Welcome To Zanesville-Muskingum County!

Thank you for requesting information about Zanesville and Muskingum County. Enclosed please find materials that will inform you about the many fine attributes and attractions of Muskingum County, Ohio – where you will find something for everyone.

Graced by rolling hills and rich woodlands, Muskingum County instills a sense of heritage, pride and well-being. Zanesville and Muskingum County are easily located right off of Interstate 70 just 55 miles east of Columbus. We offer unique shopping, fine dining, historic districts, excellent accommodations, and outdoor recreation including golfing, fishing and boating. Muskingum County is also home to the World's Largest Basket, the National Road- Zane Grey Museum, the Zanesville Art Center, the Lorena Sternwheeler, and the Wilds – a 9,000 acre wildlife preserve where you can see gazelles, wild horses, camels, rhinos and more.

Also, if antiques and pottery are your game, we have the stores for you – Hartstone, Fioriware, Robinson-Ransbottom, Friendship and Zanesville Stoneware are all made right here in our beautiful county. (Please refer to the Visitors Guide for a complete shopping list.)

The Zanesville-Muskingum County Chamber of Commerce extends its warmest welcome to you and invites you to call us for assistance anytime, 1-800-743-2303 or 740/455-8282.

Sincerely,

Kelly Ashby

Kelly Ashby
Vice-President

205 North Fifth Street – I-70 Exit · Zanesville, Ohio 43701 · (740) 452-7571

Exhibit

Summer

Winter

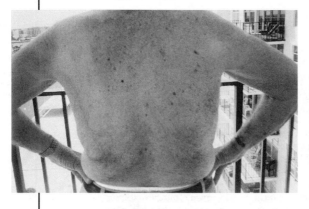

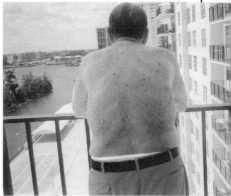

Robert Duvall
In The MALL

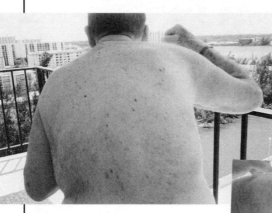

Spring

& Fall

THERE'S A LOT OF OUT THERE OUT THERE

"Is This the Line for Hanicapped Sex?"

—PHYLLIS MURPHY

560 No. Moorpark Rd.
#236
Thousand Oaks, CA 91360   USA

May 22, 1998

GOVERNMENT OF INDIA TOURIST OFFICE
BK Kakati Rd
Ulubari
Guwahati, India

Dear Tourism Office:

I am Cecil the Wanderer. I wander around, then I move on.
Sometimes I wander, sometimes I move on. My father was a wanderer
and his father was an explorer. He used to tell me "A wanderer is
just an explorer who hasn't found anything yet."

Do you have places for a wanderer to stay when he's in town?   I
need a place to wash my hands and a cot to sleep on. When I am
not sleeping or washing, I am wandering. I am Cecil the Wanderer.

Thank you for replying to me with the information I need. I have
heard your city is favorable to wanders, explorers, and sleepers.
Please send me a list of places to contact that are hospitable to
wanderers.

Sincerely,,,

Ted L. Nancy

Cecil The Wanderer

Gram : INDTOUR
Phone : 547407

GOVERNMENT OF INDIA
TOURIST OFFICE
DEPARTMENT OF TOURISM
B. K. Kakati Road, Ulubari
Guwahati-781 007

Ref. No.....Pub. 20/1/97   Date.......8.6.98.........

Dear Mr Ted,

We acknowledge with thanks the receipt of your letter dated 22.5.98 .. It was nice knowing you and better still going through your letter ,it is easily discernible from your letter that you make up for one great wanderer.

The Northeast of India becknos one like you who is on the lookout for adventure and excitement ; a vast expanse of beauty and variety. Moreover, it offers to the intending tourists an enchanting land which has attracted waves after waves of diverse human groups and has thus grown into the most colourful mosaic of ethnic,linguistic and culutral diversities. It has to be seen to be believed!

At present only three states are open to foreign tourists viz.Assam,Meghalaya and Tripura, though permits(restricted Area Permits) cabd be obtained from Indian Embassies in overseas countries.

We are sending some tourist brochures which maybe of some use to you.

The Northeast of India has so much to offer a wanderer that at the end you might finally turn an explorer.

Mr Ted L.Nancy
Cecil the Wanderer
560 No. Moorpark Rd.#236
Thousand Oaks,CA 91360 USA

yours faithfully,

(G.Ramamurthy)
Director

560 No. Moorpark Rd. #236
Thousand Oaks, CA 91360

Mar 30, 1998

Services
MOTHER NATURES ODOR REMOVER
928 Broadwater Ave.
Billings, MT 59101-2714

Dear Mother Natures Odor Remover,

I've grown an 816 pound pumpkin that is rotting in my yard. (In
Montana)   I was told that you specialize in rotting pumpkin
smells. I believe you are the company with the ad - "We
specialize in foul pumpkin odors and big, big pumpkins."   I'm at
my wits end. Can you help me with my smelly pumpkin?

Please give me a price. I want to keep the pumpkin. (If I can)
I just want to get rid of the smell. Business associates tell me
the Mother Natures Odor Remover is the best out there with
customer needs. They say that's who I should contact. I also
have other smells around the house which maybe you could look at.
I need help.

Let's get this pumpkin smell problem solved. (It's under a tarp)
Thank you for your reply. How do I set up service for you to come
out and see the problem? Someone is there in Montana at the
house, but this should be done through me. Thank you again for
your reply.

Sincerely,

Ted L. Nancy

Ted L. Nancy

MOTHER NATURE'S ODOR REMOVER®

We Don't Cover It Up... We Take It Out!
100% NATURAL-NO FRAGRANCE-NO PERFUME
ODOR- SMOKE-BACTERIA ABSORBENT
ENVIRONMENTALLY SAFE
Can be used to control virtually any odor in...

Carpet - Furniture - Floors- Air Vents- Kennels - Litter Boxes - Pet Beds - Cars - Laundry Rooms - Living Areas - Baby's Room - Offices - Restaurants - Kitchens - Nursing Rooms - Sick Rooms - Boats - Barns - Horse Barns - Fireplaces - Ashtrays - Food Storage - Clothes Closets - Refrigerators - Freezers - Gyms - Bathrooms - Hotel and Motel Rooms - Sumps, etc.. Safe to use on pets.

Here is how Odor Remover works... Airborne odors, smoke and bacteria will 'piggyback' a free ride on particles in the air, which have a positive molecular ion charge. Mother Nature's Odor Remover has a negative molecular ion charge which attracts these particles and their unwelcome riders thus ridding the immediate environment of their odoriferous effect. Mother Nature's Odor Remover's unusual longevity is a result of millions of tiny micropores that give the material a greater absorbent surface area. Mother Nature's Odor Remover comes in powder and granular form. We guarantee results and back that up with our 30-DAY MONEY-BACK guarantee if you are not happy with the results you get. Mother Nature's Odor Remover has no odor of its own, and used according to the simple directions, will eliminate the source of the odor and keep new odors from the treated area for 2 to 4 months. All that without toxicity, perfume, or fragrance. To Mother Nature's Odor Remover--Odor is Odor! The granules can be rejuvenated by placing them in the sun for one or two days. They should last for a year or more if you do this every 2 to 4 months.

MOTHER NATURE'S ODOR REMOVER APPLICATION

The area to be treated must be dry. Sprinkle the powder, sparingly, on the entire carpet. Leave it on for one hour to several days. Vacuum the entire area. If you detect an odor after a day or so, treat the area one more time. Hang one 12 oz. bag in each room. With SEVERE odor problems it may require another treatment a week or so later. Cars, RV' s etc.- Treat as above. Hang a 6 oz. bag under the dashboard and one under the seat. In an RV you would place bags evenly from front to back. Since our product is able to absorb 300% its weight in liquids, it can be used to help pick up messy spills. Sprinkle powder on the spill, wait, and then sweep or vacuum up. Use the bags in newly painted areas, the bathroom, storage rooms, closets, dressers, any area that has an odor you want removed.. Mother Nature's Odor Remover has been used in offices, apartments, classrooms, restaurants, etc.

OTHER USES

Use when planting flowers, for hydroponics, or in cat litter, the litter will last much longer. Many of you, the user, will discover other uses yourself. Even if you have no odor problem at this time, by placing one or two bags in a room, you now have 'armed' that room so new odors will not take hold for months to come. If you have an odor problem, ANYWHERE, try Mother Nature's Odor Remover FIRST! If you have tried all the cover-ups, give the job to Mother Nature's Odor Remover! After you have experienced the great results, we would appreciate it if you let your friends know. We ship Mother Nature's Odor Remover anywhere in the continental United States. We welcome your comments and would like to have you write us about them. You could use...Carpet Fresheners - Air Fresheners - A Carpet Cleaner's Service - Other odor maskers to get rid of odors, or instead, use Mother Nature' s Odor Remover 100% Natural - No Perfume -No Fragrance - Non-toxic. **MOTHER NATURE'S ODOR REMOVER ELIMINATES THE ODOR AND THE SOURCE!**

MOTHER NATURE'S ODOR REMOVER®

Mother Nature's Odor Remover will prove itself effective in many ways. It is really up to the user to test and develop uses to suit their individual needs. You too can now enjoy this fantastic, all natural, product that will do the job without covering up that odor you want to eliminate. Mother Nature's Odor Remover Will Also Save You Money! Other deodorizing sprays mask odors by covering them up with an odor all their own, and have to be frequently reapplied.

Mother Nature's Odor Remover ®
30-Day Unconditional Guarantee

All Mother Nature's Odor Remover products are sold on a 30-day money-back guarantee. If you are dissatisfied with any Mother Nature's Odor Remover product, simply return the unused portion in the original container with proof of purchase to Mother Nature' s Odor Remover for a refund. All other warranties and guarantees are expressly disclaimed and in no event shall Mother Nature's Odor Remover be liable for consequential damages.

Produced by Mother Nature

> TED -
> YES, I DO BELIEVE
> WE CAN HELP YOU WITH
> THE PUMPKIN ODOR.
> PLEASE CALL ME AT
> 800-333-7254 ASAP SO
> WE CAN DISCUSS THIS.
> SINCERELY,
> DAN DeBOER

560 No. Moorpark Rd. #236
Thousand Oaks, CA 91360

Oct 9, 1998

Mr. Dan DeBolt
MOTHER NATURES ODOR REMOVER
928 Broadwater Ave.
Billings, MT 59101

Dear Mr. DeBolt,

Thank you for writing to me. Others have told me of your
deodorizing skills. Can you help me with my pumpkin odor? It's a
big pumpkin. it smells. It's peeking out from the tarp now. What
can be done? I am still growing it It is getting bigger. It is
now 905 pounds. My pumpkin is smelly. can you help me? I believe
you advertise "Bring Us Your Biggest, Stinkiest Pumpkin. We Put A
Cover Over It And Take It Out."

Also, do you work on boat cushions?

Someone can be at the house in Montana but please address all
billings and smell problems to me in Thousand Oaks.

Are the ingredients you use safe? Will they get in the house?
Tell me about this. Thank you.

I look forward to having you get rid of my pumpkin smell. When?

Sincerely,

Ted L. Nancy

Ted L. Nancy

MOTHER NATURE'S *Odor Remover*

928 Broadwater • Billings, MT 59101
(406) 259-7254 • 1-800-333-7254 • FAX (406) 248-7235

October 21, 1998

Mr. Ted L. Nancy
560 North Moorpark Road
Thousand Oaks, CA 91360

Dear Mr. Nancy:

We have received your letter dated October 9, 1998. We would be very happy to help you with any, or all, of your odor problems. Please contact us at 1-800-333-7254 so that we can discuss this with you.

Sincerely,

Joe Steffes

JS/lh

560 No. Moorpark Rd. #236
Thousand Oaks, CA 91360

No Date. Let's keep It A Mystery

YANNI
6714 Villa Madera Dr. SW
Tacoma, Washington 98499

Dear Yanni,

I have decided I am going to model my appearance after you. I
will get long hair (I'll buy a wig) and the walrus moustache. (A
wig, but cut up). I will talk mysticism like you. You are the
man. You are Yanni. I have heard that you are changing the
spelling of your name to Yanee. Is this true? I don't like it
one bit.

I like hot dog relish. I like when they mix the mustard and the
relish together in one jar.

Can you send me another autographed picture of you? I sold mine
to a beggar. He asked me for money and I said I will SELL you my
Yanni photo. We both examined it behind his cardboard home, then
he bought it.

I desperately need another photo. Can you please sign it to Laris
Pinocchio?   Thank you, Yanni. I will write again later when I am
not so tired from the pills. Keep up this singing thing.

Sincerely,

Ted L. Nancy

YANNI

Dear Friend,

Thank you for your recent letter to Yanni. He loves hearing from all of you and, while his busy touring and recording schedules do not allow him to personally answer all the messages he receives, it is very important to him that you know how much your kind thoughts, your encouragement and your personal experiences with his music mean to him.

Yanni has asked me to add your name to his mailing list so that you will receive the Yanni International Newsletter, a quarterly update on Yanni, his touring schedule, album releases and much more. We hope you enjoy it.

Again, thank you for taking the time to write to Yanni. He really appreciates the time, emotions and thoughts you have so generously shared. In the future, please address all correspondences to Yanni to:

> YIN
> 5443 Beethoven St.
> Los Angeles, CA 90066

Yanni sends you his very best wishes and hopes to hear from you again soon.

Sincerely,

Susan Smela
Yanni Management, Inc.

Ted L. Nancy
560 N. Moorpark Rd., #236
Thousand Oaks, CA 91360
                                      Mar 31, 1997

YANNI
6714 Villa Madera Dr. SW
Tacoma, Washington 98499

Dear Yanni,

Today I went on the roof and sat there in my underpants. The roof
is tin. It is hot. I burned the back of my thighs. (Even with
underpants on). I had to put a wet wash cloth back there. It was
stinky! (Where was it?)

You are Yanni, the world's greatest mystic musician. I love your
music. I listen to it during swatting time. (Flies).

Hey, do you like butter? I mean on everything? Want to come to
my house for waffles? I make everything but the Belgian ones.

Oh, Yanni, if we could just sit on my tin roof together and eat
omelettes everything would be okay in the world. Hey, do you
think I should shave my back? It is getting awfully hairy.

Please send me ALL INFO on the Yanni FAN CLUB. I am anxious to go
to the meetings and put on clean shorts. I heard now that you
will be switching your music to oboe tunes and you will ONLY play
triple X rated accordion songs. Why? I like the Yanni music now.
I went to see you in the movie, Yanni Brasco. Where you go
undercover. You didn't look like you. But I knew it was you.
Oh, Yanni, if we could just take apart my electronic belching
machine I would be so happy.

Thank you for all the great mystic music and your accordion tunes.
They are naughty. Write me with fan club news and send me another
picture. I left the last one at a Bosco party.

Sincerely,

Ted L. Nancy
Ted L. Nancy

Y A N N I

Dear Friend,

Thank you for your recent letter to Yanni. He loves hearing from all of you and, while his current recording schedule does not allow him to answer all the messages he receives personally, he does get an opportunity to read many of them. It is very important to him that you know how much your kind thoughts, your encouragement and your personal experiences with his music mean to him.

Yanni has asked that if you are not already on the mailing list, that I add your name so that you will receive the Yanni International Newsletter, a quarterly update on Yanni, his touring schedule, album releases and much more. We hope you enjoy it.

Again, thank you for taking the time to write to Yanni. He really appreciates the emotions and thoughts you have so generously shared.

Yanni sends you his very best wishes and hopes to hear from you again soon.

Enclosed please find the autographed picture of Yanni you requested.

Sincerely,

Catherine Yatrakis
Yanni Management, Inc.

560 No. Moorpark Rd. Apt #236
Thousand Oaks, CA 91360

Apr 14, 1998

YANNI
6714 Villa Madera Dr. SW
Tacoma, Washington 98499

Dear Yanni,

Do you remember us? We are the chubby twins in body suits. (From Clovis). I barked at you. We are coming to your shows in Fritzdale and we wanted to come backstage and let you see our bonnets.

I'm wearing an Eva Gabor stretch wig right now as I write this.

Hey, Yanni, when can I get you to sign some mementos for me? They are red. One is VERY LARGE and smells like wet carpet.

Please send me an autographed picture of you. I left the last one underneath a cow and he took off with your picture on him. He ran away. He ran onto the highway and the police came and sedated him with a dart and they looked at your picture on his udder. One of the policemen said, "That's Yanni's picture on that cows belly."

Please send me more fan club news. I can't get enough. Yanni is the best! I like your new look with the orange hair and the pine cones. Belch on me.

Sincerely,

Ted L. Nancy
I Like Chimes

piano and invented a unique... still uses to this day.

World Tour Pullover
Nature's Own!
100% organically grown cotton. Travel the world or just relax in total comfort. The loose cut and plush weave are sure to make this a favorite. Featuring three-color full-front "World Tour" embroidery. Sizes M, L, XL. (Sized slightly large)
F9771 $79

Yanni Piano Folios
Feel every note as you play. Each music book features 11 different Yanni classics. **Best Of Yanni** includes "Reflections Of Passion," "First Touch," and many more classics. **In My Time** features "Enchantment," "In The Mirror" and more of Yanni's best. True collectibles!

Best Of Yanni	F9772	$14.95
In My Time	F9773	$14.95

7

560 No. Moorpark Rd.
Apt #236
Thousand Oaks, California
91360 USA

CONSULATE GENERAL OF INDIA
1990 Post Oak Blvd.
Suite 600
Houston, TX 77056   9/13/98

Dear Consulate General of India:

I have just heard the news that the Taj Mahal will now be
remodeled into a Staples Office Supply Store. Why? Can this not
be stopped? This is insanity. This is the Taj Mahal we're
talking about!!

The Taj Mahal should remain as is and not be another office supply
store. We have too many!   Will you stock Scripto pencils?

Who can assure me that this monument will continue to stand and
not be filled with paper and 3 hole punches? (Will you carry
jumbo paper clips?)

Also, when is the best time to visit the Taj Mahal and do I need a
sweater? (What about a coat?)

I look forward to hearing from you soon with this pressing
question. I want to make my trip now with my companion, Andrew.
Thank you. Please let me know what hotels are in the area.

Also can you give me the direct address to The Taj Mahal so I can
get this information? Also, do I need a visa to go to India? Let
me know. Thank you.

Respectfully,

Ted L. Nancy

Ted L. Nancy

भारत का प्रधान कोंसलावास

CONSULATE GENERAL
OF
INDIA

Hou/Com/245/10/98

October 16, 1998

Dear Mr. Nancy,

With reference to your letter dated September 13 on the remodeling of Taj Mahal into a Staples Office Supply Store, we have no such information regarding this issue. Please let us have the source of your information to clarify the matter.

Enclosed herewith is a brochure on India with tourist information, and the address of the Consulate General of India, San Francisco whom you may kindly contact for your visa as a resident of California.

Consulate General of India
540 Arguello blvd
San Fransisco,CA-94118
Tel: 415-6680683
Fax: 415-6682073

Sincerely,

Madhavi Singh
Commercial Assistant

Ted L. Nancy
560 Moorpark Rd
Thousand Oaks, CA-91360

3 Post Oak Central, Suite #600, 1990 Post Oak Blvd., Houston, Texas 77056
Tel.: (713) 626-2148 and (713) 626-2149 Fax: (713) 626-2450
E-mail: cgi-hou@accesscomm.net

560 No. Moorpark Rd. Apt #236
Thousand Oaks, CA 91360

Poetry Contest
THE POETRY
Contest

NY   May 26, 1998

Dear Poetry

I want to enter your poetry contest and win that prize! I have
been writing poetry for a long time. I think I now can win. Here
is my poem:

                "MY HATE FOR POETRY CONTESTS"

                            by

                      Ted L. Nancy

Oh how I hate poetry contests
They disgust me to no end
Those wretched poetry contests
I enter again and again
Oh how I hate poetry contests
I know I'll never win
But I know I must send
My Poem in again
And try once more to do this
Hello Darkness my old friend.

Do you like it? Can I win that prize? Let me know how far I am
in the contest.

With all the respect I have for poetry contests,

Ted L. Nancy
Ted L. Nancy

September 10, 1998

Entry: "My Hate For Poetry Contests"

Ted Nancy
560 N. Moorpark Rd.
Thousand, CA 91360

Dear Ted,

Congratulations! Your poem, *My Hate For Poetry Contests*, has been chosen for publication in one of the most unique poetry collections ever! Our Selection Committee reviewed thousands of poems, including many by new writers. The judges gave careful consideration when it came to choosing "the best" poems. Your work was selected and...

Here is your LAST CHANCE to own "My Hate For Poetry Contests"
in print **and** at incredible savings!

With a limited amount of "publishing space" remaining, this offer is going out on a first-come, first-served basis. This is the same high-quality book that was previously offered at $59.95. Now, I am offering you your own copy for ONLY $49.95.

This unique compilation of poems brings together the collected works of today's promising poets. This brilliant anthology has hundreds of archival quality pages brimming with verse, and its classic hardbound cover is richly tooled with a gleaming gold-leaf design. *My Hate For Poetry Contests* truly belongs in this generously-sized deluxe volume.

Ted, so many people wish they had copies of the book in which their poem appears, but miss the chance. Don't let this pass you by. Just return the enclosed rush-order form today. You risk nothing.

Yours Sincerely

P.S.   Your satisfaction is guaranteed. If you are unsatisfied for any reason, you may return your book for a full and prompt refund.

P.P.S.   Orders will be filled on a first-come, first-served basis. I'm sorry, there can be no exceptions. Please see your rush-order form for details.

Congratulations, Ted, on being a semifinalist in our Poetry Contest! Your poem, "My Hate For Poetry Contests," has been entered into our final competition.

Dear Ted,

Congratulations on your acceptance of "My Hate For Poetry Contests" by The Poetry   ! You, Ted, are closer than ever to winning the $1,000 Grand Prize (or one of 99 Honorable Mention Awards). Within a few weeks, our judges will choose the Finalists and decide on a winner.

So many of our new poets have expressed their joy in being a poet. But you've also told us how important it is to share your poems with others. After all, what's the point of writing poetry at all ... if it can't be read and felt by those people who are most important to you?

We couldn't agree more. And so The Poetry wants to give you a special opportunity, Ted, to both celebrate — and share — your work. We've put together a very special edition for you — one which features your poem, "My Hate For Poetry Contests," and also makes a perfect gift. It's called   *Poets: Edition.*

A Special Place for "My Hate For Poetry Contests,"...

Sincerely,

for the Poetry

560 No Moorpark Rd. Apt #236
Thousand Oaks, CA 91360

Poetry Contest
THE POETRY

NY   Oct 8, 1998

Dear Poetry

I want to enter your contest again. I am refining my poem that I
have entered before. It is now to where I want it. I really have
it down. Here it is:

"WHY I REALLY HATE POETRY CONTESTS"

by

Ted L. Nancy

Oh how I really hate poetry contests
They keep sending you crap through the mail
Oh I can't stand to receive junk from poetry contests anymore
They turn my stomach to no end
Oh these stupid poetry contests
They just want you to buy their book
I have to make a doody now
Hello darkness my old friend
I am the poetry man
I just want to go to the trash and chuck it
There was an old lady from Nantucket
I am so sick of poetry contests
You have no idea
I can rhyme orange
If I use car hinge

Do you like it? Let me know when I can get my prize. Do you
still give out floppy blimps?

Sincerely,

Ted L. Nancy
Ted L. Nancy

POETRY

Entry: "Why I Really Hate Poetry Contests"

Ted Nancy
560 N Moorpark Rd Apt 236
Thousand Oaks, CA 91360

January 8, 1999

Dear Ted,

Congratulations! Your poem, *Why I Really Hate Poetry Contests*, has been selected as one of our contest semifinalists! You, Ted, may win the $1,000 Grand Prize, or one of the 69 other prizes! Included with this letter are "Contest Guidelines" and a complete explanation of prizes to be awarded.

Our Selection Panel has been hard at work reviewing thousands of poems, including a number of them by new writers. Our panel will make their final decision within the next month. The judges give careful consideration when it comes to choosing "the best" poems. We are firmly committed to discovering and showcasing the best talent.

Your poem, *Why I Really Hate Poetry Contests*, has been accepted based on its originality and creativity.

Ted, we'd be proud to publish *Why I Really Hate Poetry Contests* in our upcoming anthology. This may be the most unique poetry collection ever published. It will be a generous-sized, deluxe volume of collected works by some of today's most promising authors. This treasured anthology will contain several hundred "museum-quality" printed pages and will be exquisitely hardbound in a beautifully crafted cover, featuring original full-color artwork. It will no doubt become the center of conversation among friends and family.

You risk nothing...

Why I Really Hate Poetry Contests is a unique extension of you. It is a special and purposeful creation that will live forever. I guarantee you'll be proud of it.

Once again, we wish to congratulate you on being one of our contest semifinalists.

Yours sincerely,

P.S. We are proud to publish fine poems such as yours in our upcoming edition. As a semifinalist, now is the time to order your own copy including your poem, *Why I Really Hate Poetry Contests*. Time is of the essence; we must hear from you by February 12, 1999.

The International Library of Poetry

1 Poetry Plaza • Owings Mills, Maryland 21117-6282 • (410) 356-2000 • www.poetry.com

VIP# P1564706-801

January 29, 1999

Wonderful verse!
Select for the "Sound of Poetry"
— CS

Ted Nancy
560 N Moorpark Rd Apt 236
Thousand Oaks, CA 91360

Re: <u>The Radiance of Summer Sun</u>

This publisher's proof represents your poem as it is now scheduled to appear in print. Please carefully review the publisher's proof . . . check carefully for typographical errors . . . indicate any changes directly on the proof, and return it to us in the enclosed envelope. If your poem is correct as is, please initial the proof and return it without changes. <u>Please note that you must certify the accuracy of this proof by making appropriate changes.</u> Only initial the proof if everything is correct. By returning this proof, you authorize us to publish your poem with corrections, if necessary, as indicated below.

NOTE: *This proof must be returned postmarked no later than* **February 26, 1999,** *so we can make our scheduled publication date. Poems must be 20 lines or less. Only one entry per contestant.*

Why I Really Hate Poetry Contests

Oh how I really hate poetry contest
They keep sending you crap through the mail
Oh I can't stand to receive junk from poetry contests anymore
They turn my stomach to no end
Oh these stupid poetry contests
They just want you to buy their book
I have to make a doody now
Hello darkness my old friend
I am the poetry man
I just want to go to the trash and chuck it
There was an old lady from Nantucket
I am so sick of poetry contests
You have no idea
I can rhyme orange
If I use car hinge

Ted L. Nancy

```
                              560 No. Moorpark Rd. Apt #236
                              Thousand Oaks, CA 91360
```

Poetry Contest
THE POETRY

        NY 1   Apr 2, 1999

Dear Poetry

I want to enter your contest for a third time. I am really close
to winning. I feel it. Here is my poem:

        "WHY I'M GOING TO JUMP OFF A 30 STORY BUILDING
           BECAUSE OF YOUR POETRY CONTESTS"

                          by

                     Ted L. Nancy

Oh I'm going to jump off a building because of your poetry contest
I can't take any more of your mail to me
Oh I shake every time your junk comes to my door
I'm going to throw myself off a big building
Down Down Down
Down to the floor
Because of you
I will jump. This is the end
I will splatter all over like a cream pie
Then it surely will be
Hello Darkness My Old Friend

Do you like it? I think for sure now I win that contest. Let me
know.

With Resect For Poetry and Their Contests,

Ted L. Nancy

P.S. Could you please leave a mattress on the sidewalk! Thank
you.

poetry

October 15, 1999

Ted Nancy
560 No Moorpark Rd Apt 236
Thousand Oaks CA 91360

Dear Ted,

After carefully reading and discussing your poem, our Selection Committee has certifed your poem as a semi-finalist in our North American Open Poetry Contest. Your poem will automatically be entered into the final competition held in December 1999. As a semi-finalist, you now have an excellent chance of winning one of 114 cash or gift prizes -- including the $1,000.00 Grand Prize. You may even win the $10,000.00 annual Grand Prize! We wish you the best of luck as you compete for these prizes in the coming weeks (a complete list of prizes is enclosed).

And that's not all...

Ted...Imagine Your Poem
Featured in a Beautiful Coffee-table Edition!

In celebration of the unique talent that you have displayed, we also wish to <u>publish your poem</u> in what promises to be one of the most highly sought after collections of poetry we have ever published...

Sun

Library of Congress ISBN-1-

___Sun_____, scheduled for publication in Winter 2000, will be a classic, coffee-table quality hardbound volume -- printed on fine-milled paper specifically selected to last for generations. It will make a handsome addition to any library, a treasured family keepsake, or a highly valued personal gift.

NO OBLIGATION WHATSOEVER

Before going any further, Ted, let me make one thing clear ... your poem was selected for publication, and as a contest semi-finalist, on the basis of your unique talent and artistic vision. We believe it will add to the importance and appeal of this edition. *In this regard, you are under no obligation whatsoever to submit any entry fee, any subsidy payment, or to make any purchase of any kind.* Of course, many people do wish to own a copy of the anthology in which their artistry appears. If this is the case, we welcome your order -- and guarantee your satisfaction. Please see the enclosed material for special discount information if you would like to acquire a copy of ___Sun._____,

Again, congratulations, Ted. We feel you have a special talent and look forward to the publication of your poem in ___Sun_____.

Sincerely,

P.S.   Ted, you should be genuinely proud of your accomplishment. Of the thousands of poems we read each year, only a fraction can be published. We are pleased that "Why I'm Going to Jump Off a 30 Story Building Because of Your Poetry" will appropriately achieve the recognition that a national publication can give it. And, if you order ___Sun_____, we are so confident that you will love both the quality of the edition and the way your poem is presented, we can proudly offer an unconditional money back guarantee. If for any reason you are dissatisfied, your money will be promptly refunded.

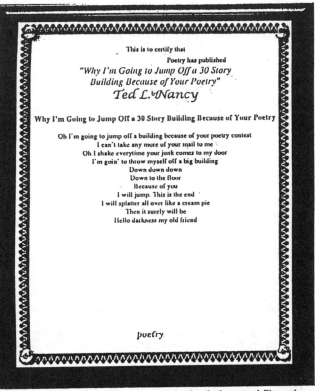

This is to certify that

Poetry has published

"Why I'm Going to Jump Off a 30 Story Building Because of Your Poetry"

Ted L. Nancy

Why I'm Going to Jump Off a 30 Story Building Because of Your Poetry

Oh I'm going to jump off a building because of your poetry contest
I can't take any more of your mail to me
Oh I shake everytime your junk comes to my door
I'm goin' to throw myself off a big building
Down down down
Down to the floor
Because of you
I will jump. This is the end
I will splatter all over like a cream pie
Then it surely will be
Hello darkness my old friend

poetry

Your complete poem will be beautifully mounted and perfectly centered. Plaque above is for illustration purposes only. Actual size is 10½" x 13", much larger than shown.

If you have previously submitted editorial changes, they WILL be included on your plaque and in the book. If you have new editorial changes, please indicate them directly on this form.

I'M A PEEPHOLE PERSON

"Go Pound Sand Up Your Nostril"
My Dad at Dinner

560 No. Moorpark Rd. #236
Thousand Oaks, CA 91360

Decorator Dept.
GILFORD CUSTOM WALLPAPER
3001 Hamburg Pike
Jeffersonville, IN 47130   3/12/98

Dear Gilford Wallpapers,

A friend of mine showed me your 1998 Ned Beatty wallpaper
patterns. I would like to order mine immediately. I am redoing
my entire house – 3600 square feet – in Ned Beatty wallpaper. It
will be magnificent! Also what is the best way to strip our
Charles Durning wallpaper from the wall? Or can we apply the Ned
Beatty wallpaper right over the Charles Durning? It's on tight.

Is Bill still around? What about Howie? Your company is highly
recommended and I have called there before and was happy with
Howie.

My Charles Durning wallpaper has been on my walls for 55 months.
The face has retained its gloss, but there is some peeling by his
feet. Now it is time for a complete redo of wallpaper in my home.
The entire home should be re-wallpapered in the Ned Beatty
pattern. I understand there are 5 action shots of Ned including
bending.

Should I make an appointment or just come in? Is Howie still
there? I have heard your wallpaper company has the BEST customer
service in California. That's what I heard. And I will continue
to hear that! Let me know who I talk to about redoing my entire
home with new wallpaper. Who do I talk to about getting this
custom wallpaper made? Is there a dealer you can lead me to? I
look forward to hearing from you soon. Thank you.

Sincerely,

Ted L. Nancy

Metropolitan Louisville

3001 Hamburg Pike
Jeffersonville, IN 47130

Mr. Ted L. Nancy
560 No. Moorpark Rd. Apt #236
Thousand Oaks, CA 91360

91360+3760 |||...||..||.||.|.||....||..|.||.||...||.||..||.|

560 No. Moorpark Rd. Apt #236
Thousand Oaks, CA 91360

Customer Service Dept.
Gilford Custom Wallcoverings
3001 Hamburg Pike
Jeffersonville, IN 47130

Dear Customer Service Department:

I wrote to you some time ago and requested information on if you could make custom made wallpaper for my home. I want to redo my entire home in a special pattern and I was wondering if you made this wallpaper? I did not hear back from you.

I was wondering if there was a Howie working there? Is he still there? If not could you let me know who I write to regarding getting this custom made wallpaper. It would have a picture of a face on it. Thank you. I look forward to your reply. I have heard that your company makes custom wallpaper or could tell em who does. And I have heard that you have an excellent company. Thank you once again.

Sincerely,

Ted L. Nancy

UPHOLSTERY · PANEL FABRICS · WALLCOVERINGS · FLOORCOVERINGS

Representatives in:
Atlanta
Baton Rouge
Boston
Buffalo
Charlotte
Chicago
Cincinnati
Cleveland
Connecticut
Dallas
Denver
Detroit
Honolulu
Houston
Jacksonville
Kansas City
Los Angeles
Las Vegas
Lexington
Louisville
Miami
Minneapolis
Mississippi
Nashville
New Jersey
New York City
Orlando
Philadelphia
Phoenix
Pittsburgh
Rhode Island
Rochester
Sacramento
St. Louis
San Antonio
San Diego
San Francisco
Seattle
Washington D.C.
Calgary
London
Melbourne
Montreal
Mexico
San Juan
Seoul
Singapore
Toronto
Vancouver

May 19, 1998

Mr. Ted L. Nancy
560 No. Moorpark Rd. Apt. #236
Thousand Oaks, CA 91360

Dear Mr. Nancy,

I've received your letter requesting information on custom wallpaper. You are correct in that Gilford does produce custom wallcovering, I do not know however if I can help you with your particular request. I would need to know more about what you are wanting. Measurements are required on the area you intend to cover and more details as to the type of design and construction you need.

We have no one here named Howie, but if you would like to call me I'd be happy to try and help you.

Sincerely,

Dick Wallingford
Vice President

DW:ej

Enclosure

Metropolitan Louisville

3001 Hamburg Pike
Jeffersonville, IN 47130

Office: 812-288-7900
Fax: 812-288-0872
Toll Free: 1-800-852-5454

560 No. Moorpark Rd. Apt #236
Thousand Oaks, CA 91360

Mar 21, 1998

U.S. ARMY RECRUITING STATION
9673 Sierra Ave.
Fontana, CA 92335-2424

Dear U.S. Army:

I am a 57 year old 2 foot man ready to serve my country any way I
can. I am Pip The Mighty Squeak - former circus star, sideshow
performer, and current video store employee.

I want information on how I can join the United States Army. I am
ready to serve in the camel-cow experiment. I am ready to become
an officer or do whatever for you. (Need teeth fixed does Army do
this?)

I am Pip The Mighty Squeak! Perhaps you have heard of me. I did
an act where I lifted a shoe over my head. I am moving to Fontana
soon. I want to be in the Army and live on a bunk. Please tell
me how I join up. I am very tiny but can be of use. I know the
video world inside and out. Have rented out "The Crow" over 1,000
times. Am anxious. Thank you, U.S. Army. Let's get me in
uniform! I want a hat. Send me info.

Sincerely,

Ted L. Nancy

Ted L. Nancy
Pip The Mighty Squeak

Dear Ted,

Confidence, self-discipline, determination and team spirit are the qualities that have propelled successful people to the top of their professions. The Army can help you develop these same successful traits and give you the edge you need to get ahead in today's competitive job market.

Check out the career training the Army offers.

* You can choose from one of more than 200 Military Occupational Specialties, many of which have civilian counterparts like computer programming, aviation or law enforcement. When you qualify, the training you select will be guaranteed in writing.

* If the training you select isn't immediately available, you can lock in a future school date up to one full year in advance through our Delayed Entry Program.

Another important Army advantage is money for college. If you qualify for the Montgomery GI Bill plus the Army College Fund, in just four years you can accumulate up to $40,000 for college or technical school.

If you'd like to have a challenging, rewarding career - get-on-the-job training and experience, money for college, and even more benefits, then find out more about Army opportunities. With the right attitude, training and education, there's no limit to what you can accomplish.

Sincerely

David Douglass
Staff Sergeant
United States Army Recruiter

P.S. Act FAST! Mail the enclosed reply card TODAY!

ARMY
BE ALL YOU CAN BE.

560 No. Moorpark Rd. #236
Thousand Oaks, CA 91360

Apr 27, 1999

Manager
BIRKENSTOCK COMFORT SHOES
6323 El Cajon Blvd.
San Diego, CA 92115

Dear Birkenstock Comfort Shoes:

I am 11 inches tall and weigh 41 pounds. My Name is Beto The
Wonder Squeak, part of the performing Squeak family. (Pip is
estranged). I perform a 45 minute act where I dance around, shout
out bar b que orders, rope a turtle, and generally be amusing.

I am booking my Midwest schedule now and need 20 pairs of clogs
for this tour. I understand you have clogs for my feet. How
much?

I have 100 tiny bandaids on my buttocks from an industrial
accident. I am Beto the Wonder Squeak! World's tiniest man who
wears a hat and barks out menu items! Please include this on all
posters, and car windshield flyers! Thank you. Hey. what is the
capitol of Rangoon? Do you know?

I look forward to information about my clogs. How do we get these
clogs to me? Who do I speak to? Is there a brochure? I have
wide feet. I need shoes. Can you suggest something?

Sincerely,

Ted L. Nancy
Beto The Wonder Squeak

4/29/99

Dear Ted, Beto the Wonder Squeak,

our shoes are great! The clogs are $103.<u>95</u> they come in <u>all</u> sizes.

please call us to order 619-583-4761

and no there is no Capital of Rangoon. Rangoon is a Capital I'm told by my boss.

Let us know how we can assist you. Send us a tracing of your feet on paper if you want.

Greetings From The folks at Birkenstock

BIRKENSTOCK ®
OF SAN DIEGO
6323 EL CAJON BLVD.
SAN DIEGO, CA 92115
(619) 583-4761

560 No. Moorpark Rd. Apt #236
Thousand Oaks, CA 91360 USA

Apr 24, 1999

Information
TONGA VISITORS BUREAU
Ha'apai Branch
P.O. Box 60
Pangai, Ha'apai
Tonga

Dear Tonga Visitors Bureau.

Perhaps you can help me.

I am looking for Pet Barf. I believe you sell this German product
in your Tonga gift shops. Can I order a tin? I believe the name
is Captain Reedy's Pet Barf.

Growing up in Germany I remember it, this Pet Barf under the
Christmas tree. There was nothing better then looking under that
tree and seeing Pet Barf.

Can you give me a list of some Tonga gift shops that I may find
this product at? Good to see it back in stores after a 2 year
ban. Thank you.

Sincerely,

Ted L. Nancy

Ted L. Nancy

The Kingdom of
Tonga
ancient polynesia

TONGA VISITORS BUREAU, P.O. Box 37, Nuku'alofa TONGA, South Pacific, Ph : (676) 25 334, Fx : (676) 23507
http://www.vacations.tvb.gov.to, Email.tvb@kalianet.to

28th July 1999

Dear Ted L. Nancy,

Malo e lelei and warm greetings from the Island of Ha'apai -Kingdom of Tonga!

Apologies for not answering to you as per requested.

About the Department stores, please find enclose the list for them and since I'll be here for the next two weeks I'll be glad to help you with the sorting of gifts wanted to purchase for your employees.

I suggest that you do your shopping from the Friendly Islands Bookshop, Langafonua Handicraft Shop, FIMCO handicraft and gift shop, Micky Guttenbeil's gift shop and the Dateline Duty Free shop or the Leiola Duty free shop.

If you have any email address please do let me know so that our communication will be quicker and easier. Do find enclose some information on Tonga and the best time to visit to Tonga is from January - December (all year weather). Our email here in Ha'apai is: tvbhp@kalianet.to or you can check our web site: http://www.vacations.tvb.gov.to

For further information please do write back.

Regards,

Mele T-L Tukia
Assistant Information Officer

North America
4605 Driftwood Court
El Sobrante
CA 94108-1805
Ph: (510) 223 13181
Fx: (510) 758 627
Email:tonga@value.net

Australia
642 King St
Newtown, Sydney
NSW 2042
Ph: (612) 9550 4711
Fx: (9519 9419

New Zealand
PO Box 24-054
Royal Oak
Auckland
Ph: (649) 634 1519
Fx: (649) 636 8973

PATA

TCSP

560 No. Moorpark Rd. #236
Thousand Oaks, CA 91360

Dec 9, 1996

Customer Service Dept.
DEGREE DEODORANT
C/O Helene Curtis Co.
325 N. Wells St.
Chicago, IL 60610

Dear Degree Deodorant,

I have been using your product for some time and am quite happy
with it. My underarms are now finally back to normal! I have
used your deodorant for every day functions as well as special
events. (Like at a buffet). I have never had the occasion to
feel embarrassed at all.

My question to you is that on the back of your Degree
Antipersirant it says that your deodorant "Keeps Your Underarms
Cool And Dry."

Then I look at a package of Rigatoni Parmesan cheese and it says
"Store In A Cool Dry Place."

What gives? I'm confused. Should I store my Parmesan cheese
under my arms? Would it be safe to spray Degree on my cheese
and put my cheese anywhere? I am asking Degree because you make
the BEST deodorant out there. I will use no others. Degree is
the best at keeping underarms dry AND at storing. I tell
everyone about it when we wash.

Could you send me a list of your deodorant sizes so I can buy
the best size for me and not share it? Thank you, Degree, the
best at underarm care for a long time now. I look forward to
hearing from you soon. Send me a picture of your deodorant for
my wall. Thank you.

Sincerely,

Ted L. Nancy

Ted L. Nancy

Helene Curtis, Inc.
800 Sylvan Avenue
Englewood Cliffs, New Jersey
07632
Telephone 1-800-621-2013

Consumer Services

December 20, 1996

Mr. Ted L. Nancy   CE 3724011A
560 N Moorpark Road
Thousand Oaks, CA 91360

Dear Mr. Nancy:

It was thoughtful of you to let us hear your comments about Degree.

For many years, our company has been making every effort to provide consumers with superior products to meet their individual needs and preferences. Comments such as yours are certainly gratifying - and most welcome.

As a token of our appreciation, I am enclosing a coupon for your use. If we can be of service in the future, please contact us.

Sincerely,

Chris Greene
Consumer Representative

cig/ww
Enclosure

560 No. Moorpark Rd. Apt #236
Thousand Oaks, CA 91360 USA

Apr 5, 1999

Room Reservations
ASTORIA HOTEL
39 Bolshaya Morskaya ul.
St Petersburg, Russia

Dear Astoria Hotel:

I need a room for 3 nights. June 1, 2, 3, 1999. Your finest
accomodations. I may need a security guard to guard my every
move. Even while sleeping.

I am an X Rated porno star that looks like Roy Clark. I am 5'5"
245 pounds with large bushy sideburns. I look EXACTLY like the
country western singer as if he were performing in adult films.
Close your eyes and imagine Roy's face squinched up making mule
bellows. Think of his eyelids fluttering and veins popping on his
forehead. Think of Roy Clark at the moment of ecstasy, he's
aroused and his eyes are bulging out, his face is red and he's out
of his mind. That's me. My latest adult movie is "Roy Clark
Look-alike Pickin' And Grinnin."

How can I be sure I will not be accosted by females when I check
in to your 12 star hotel? (I have seen pictures of it in shoe
magazines)

Please let me know how much the room is for June 1-3, 1999. I
have heard that you have the finest hotel in Russia and that you
cater to Roy Clark look-alikes who do saucy adult films. Also,
can I check in with my own sink?

Sincerely,

Ted L. Nancy

ASTORIA & D'ANGLETERRE
HOTELS
ST. PETERSBURG

Mr. Ted L. Nancy

560 No.Moorpark Rd. Apt #236
Thousand Oaks, CA 91360 USA

Dear Mr. Nancy,

Thank you very much for showing interest in our Hotel.
I'm extremely sorry but we are not able to accommodate you for the period
requested. Unfortunately we are already fully booked for the beginning of June.
I hope we will have an opportunity to welcome you in our hotel next time in the
future.
Hope for your understanding.

Sincerely,

Irene Stepanova
Reservations Supervisor

ЯF
HOTELS
Rocco Forte's new Hotel Group

39, Bolshaya Morskaya, St.Petersburg, 190000, Russia Tel: +7 812 210 5757 Fax: +7 812 210 5059

ОАО "Г.К.Астория", Россия, 190000 С.-Петербург, ул. Большая Морская, 39
р/с № 40702810100000000563 в ОАО "АБ Россия",
к/с 30101810800000000861, ИНН 7830002896, ОКОНХ 90220, ОКПО 02573390, БИК 044030861

560 No. Moorpark Rd. Apt. #236
Thousand Oaks, California 91360   USA

PRESIDENT VACLAV HAVEL
Hradecek
CZ-11908 Praha
Czech Republic   May 6, 1998

Dear Honorable President Havel,

This is just a note to tell you how much respect I have for you
and how our club respects the way you have handled yourself in the
dignified manner you have over the years. I am happy to announce
that we have bestowed membership on you in the Thousand Oaks
Vacuum Club. We want you to be our Honorary Treasurer. We want
to send you money for our club. This is sponsored by Markel Pest
Control (serving Thousand Oaks for 16 months now)

As our Treasurer we want to include you at all company meetings,
membership drives, and car washes. We want you to advise us on
what to do with our money. We feel that you as a great leader in
Czechoslovakia have led the people for many years and have done
this graciously and tirelessly.   We now want you to do the same
for us. (Lead us graciously)

Take our money and invest it. Buy whatever you want. If you
think swimsuit netting is the answer then buy it up! Where should
I send the check? How do I give this money to you? What
denominations would you like? You are the finest leader I have
ever read about and your lifestyle has certainly shown our members
that you know what to do with our money. Buy ironing board covers
if you have to. I don't care.

And don't forget, Markel is the best at getting rid of Pumpkin
odor. I look forward to my reply from you. Thank you, President
Havel, for being a fine leader and a nice man. Your dignity
stands as an endorsement to those less dignified.

With All The Respect I Have,

Ted L. Nancy

Ted L. Nancy
Please send me a signed picture of you for my wall.

Kancelář prezidenta republiky

May 27, 1998

Dear Ted,

President Václav Havel appreciates your appointment him the Honorary Treasurer of your Thousand Oaks Vaccum Club. Unfortunately it is impossible for him to give time to any other activity apart from those required of him as Head of State. Thank you on his behalf for your interest.

Enclosed please find his autographed photo.

With best regards,

Vladimír Hanzel
Personal Secretary to the President

Ted l. Nancy
560 No. Moorpark Rd. Apt. 236
Thousand Oaks, California 91360
USA

Office of the President
Czech Republic
CZ-119 08 Praha-Hrad
Tel.: (420/2) 2437 1111, Fax: (420/2) 2437 3300

560 No. Moorpark Rd. Apt #236
Thousand Oaks, CA 91360 USA

PRESIDENT VACLAV HAVEL
Office Of The President
Hradecek
CZ-119 08 Praha-Hrad
Czech Republic

STILL WAITING FOR REPLY

Apr 2, 1999

Dear Honorable President Havel,

I want to tell you how dignified I think you are. The Thousand
Oaks Vacuum Club feels you are the finest leader in the world
today. You have led graciously and tirelessly.

For that reason we want to name our new vacuum cleaner after you -
The Havel 2000. This vacuum cleaner can pick up dirt near the
edge of the carpet and has a 6 inch drape attachment. It can
scoop dog balls (hairs) before they settle into the carpet. You
deserve this honor!

A certificate is forthcoming.

You have led the Czech Republic with dignity and grace. The Havel
2000 can empty its bag by itself. You have been a tireless world
leader. The Havel 2000 can pick cat fur off drapes with a plastic
attachment. You are a respected President that has shown
exemplary diligence and utter restraint. The Havel 2000 comes in
3 colors. (Working on blue)

We want this honor to dignify you. Perhaps a picture of your face
can go on the cushion odorizer spritz? Let us know. Will vacuum
over frog munch.

Could you send us an autographed picture for our buffet?

Thank you President Havel for your many achievements: President
of the Czech Republic and now having the The Havel 2000 Vacuum
Cleaner named after you. The Thousand Oaks Vacuum Club is proud
to have you for a leader. We look forward to hearing from you
soon with our picture.

All My Respect,

Ted L. Nancy

560 No. Moorpark Rd. Apt #236
Thousand Oaks, CA 91360

Head Committee
MOUNT RUSHMORE NATIONAL MEMORIAL SOCIETY
Box 1524
Rapid City, SD 57709-1524   Dec 6, 1996

Dear Mount Rushmore,

I am writing to you because I have just heard the fantastic good
news. I am so excited that you will be putting the head of Lou
Rawls on Mount Rushmore.

I think this is long overdue. Lou Rawls is the perfect head to
put on your rock monument next to Washington, Jefferson, Lincoln,
and Theodore Roosevelt. Bravo! (Him or Otis Rush).

I want to be there during the carving ceremony. Let's bring this
great American to the top of the mountain where he deserves to be.
I love his "Groovy People" song on the "All Things In Time" Album.
And the title of that album has certainly now come true! Gutzon
Borglum would be proud.

Thank you, Mount Rushmore, for this great decision. You are to be
commended. Applause!

Also, do you sell pie in the cafeteria? I am visiting soon and
need to know if you have any kind of meringue pies over there?

Please write me and let me know you are in receipt of my letter
and all have been thanked. Thank you. Remember, 5 heads are
better than 4. (My father used to say that to me all the time).

I look forward to hearing from you with cafeteria visiting hours.
Thank you.

Sincerely,

Ted L. Nancy

United States Department of the Interior

NATIONAL PARK SERVICE
MOUNT RUSHMORE NATIONAL MEMORIAL
KEYSTONE, SOUTH DAKOTA 57751-0268

IN REPLY
REFER TO:

February 20, 1997

Ted L. Nancy
560 No. Moorpark RD.. Apt #236
Thousand Oaks, CA 91360

Dear Mr. Nancy:

Thank you for your letter suggesting adding another figure to Mount Rushmore National Memorial.

Your suggestion long with many others have been suggested on numerous occasions since the completion of the Memorial.

There have been serious requests that consideration be given to Presidents Franklin Roosevelt and John F. Kennedy. There have also been some not so serious proposals to add Clark Gable, John Wayne or Mickey Mouse. The truth is that all the granite suitable for carving another colossal head has been used in the present design. There is no more stone available to carve another figure.

The sculpture on Mount Rushmore is considered to be a work of art; the fruit of the genius of Sculptor Gutzon Borglum. Many hands aided in the project; but his vision was the guiding light. As a work of art; it is protected and preserved by the National Park Service and remains as an inspirational work of American creative ability.

Sincerely,

James G. Popovich
Chief of Interpretation

560 No. Moorpark Rd. Apt #236
Thousand Oaks, CA 91360

Jul 20, 1999

Submissions
SANDLAPPER MAGAZINE
The Magazine Of South Carolina
The Sandlapper Society
P.O. Box 1108
Lexington, SC 29071

Dear Sandlapper Magazine:

I have heard that you are looking for interesting photos for your
magazine.

I have a photo of Leonardo DiCaprio with no shirt on. I was at
the mall when I saw Leonardo DiCaprio. I asked him to take his
shirt off and bend forward. He did. Then we both went to see
"Titanic" together at the Cineplex 17. (I ate Sweet Tarts. And I
gave him one. He tasted it and went "phooey and spit it out on
the floor).

I would like to put my picture of Leonardo DiCaprio bending
forward in your magazine. Do you want to see it? I have to admit
you can see the top of Leonardo DiCaprio's underpants in the
picture. Female fans will want to see this picture. I showed it
to one girl and she fainted. How do I send it to you? I hope
this is Leonardo DiCaprio. He said it was him and we both had
Sweet Tarts together. It sure looks like him. Let me know when
you see the photo. Thank you. I look forward to hearing from you
soon to show you my photo of (what I believe is) Leonardo
DiCaprio. I have always considered myself a Sandlapper, if only
in spirit.

Sincerely,

Ted L. Nancy

Sandlapper®

The Magazine of South Carolina

September 8, 1999

Mr. Ted L. Nancy
560 North Moorpark Road, #236
Thousand Oaks, CA 91360

Dear Mr. Nancy:

My memory is faulty, but I do remember your letter and believe that since I can't find it, I must have responded. Oh well.

The long and short of it is, we may be interested in celebrity photos if the celebrities are from South Carolina. The enclosed guidelines should give you more information about what we are, how we operate and what we pay.

Please call, write or e-mail (aida@sandlapper.org) if you have any questions. Sorry for the mix-up.

Sincerely,

Aida Rogers
associate editor

P.O. Box 1108, Lexington, SC 29071 ◆ phone (803) 359-9941 ◆ fax (803) 359-0629 ◆ http://vvvv.sandlapper.org

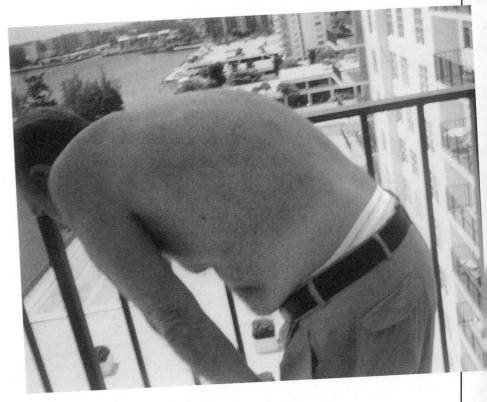

Leonardo DiCaprio
(I Think it's him)
bending Forward

Sandlapper Society, Inc.

Post Office Box 1108
Lexington, SC 29071

SEP 8 '99
S.C.

US POSTAGE
≈ 0.33
F METER
2914212

Mr. Ted L. Nancy
560 North Moorpark Road #236
Thousand Oaks, CA 91360

560 No Moorpark Rd.   Apt #236
Thousand Oaks, CA 91360

Aug 10, 1999

Popeye Information
CHESTER ILLINOIS CHAMBER OF COMMERCE
1 Taylor
Chester Illinois 62233

Dear Chester Illinois Chamber Of Commerce:

I understand that Chester, Illinois is home to Popeye. That you
have everything Popeye in your fine community. That Popeye is
King. Why shouldn't he be? I am a long time Popeye admirer. My
3rd child is named Popeye and she has adjusted nicely. Can you
give me information on any Popeye Events you are holding? Don't
hold back.

Is there still a Popeye floating contest?   Do you sell Chicken
Popeye in the cafeteria?   I once had Chicken Pox Pie. Do you
have anything honoring Bluto? What about in the next town over?
What's going on there?   What about the Popeye Millennium? Popeye
2000 is coming on fast.

When is your Popeye weekend this year? Will you have 3 legged
Popeye races? My cleaning lady looks like Popeye. She dusts very
good. There is nobody finer then Popeye the Sailor Man. The city
of Chester Illinois should be proud and chest popping that they
have adopted Popeye as their leader.

Will you have whistling events? Nudge my lizard. When is Jimmy
Fest? And will you sell Jelly Watches? Where can I change a tire
in Chester? This is a must!

I look forward to information on any Popeye events, Popeye
romantic weekend getaways, Popeye sandwiches. Let's get it on!

Respectfully,

Ted L. Nancy
Ted L. Nancy

Chester Chamber of Commerce

CHESTER, ILLINOIS

'Home of Popeye'

HISTORIC SITES

Pierre Menard Home, "The Mt. Vernon of the West"
Fort Kaskaskia, Overlooking Kaskaskia Island
Governor Shadrach Bond State Memorial
U.S. Senator Elias Kent Kane Memorial
The Liberty Bell of the West
Mary's River Covered Bridge
Popeye Statue

August 31, 1999

Mr. Ted Nancy
560 N. Moorpark Road
#236
Thousand Oaks, CA. 91360

Dear Mr. Nancy,

Here is a business card from our Popeye store in town. We have also enclosed an event schedule for this years picnic.

Spinach Can Collectibles
"THE POPEYE SHOP"
- Memorabilia - Souvenirs -
- Comics - Cards - Collectibles -
- Mail Order Catalog -
TOURIST INFORMATION CENTER
1001 State - Chester, Illinois - 62233
(618)826-4567 - FAX 826-2809
VISA - MASTERCARD - DISCOVER
©King Features Syndicate
"OFFICIAL POPEYE FANCLUB HEADQUARTERS"

Thank you,

CHESTER CHAMBER OF COMMERCE

"On the Banks of the Beautiful Mississippi River"
Chester Chamber of Commerce
P.O. Box 585
Chester, IL 62233
(618) 826-2721

Chester, Illinois' 20th Annual

Popeye's Picnic

"Popeye's Mardi Gras"

Thursday, September 9 1999

6:30 pm	BBQ For All Sponsors at Cole Memorial Park

Friday, September 10, 1999

4:00 pm	Stands & Carnival Rides Open (Picnic Grounds)
5:00 pm - 8:00 pm	McMurtry's Petting Zoo (Picnic Area)
5:30 pm - 8:30 pm	Washer Tournament (Check-in 5 pm) (Across from K of C Hall)
7:15 pm - 7:45 pm	Performance by "The Dance Company" (Chester Square)
8:00 pm	Prince/Princess Coronation (Chester Square)
8:00 pm	Dance — "Cosmo T" (VFW Parking Lot)
9:00 pm - 11:00 pm	Teen Dance - DJ (Picnic Area)
9:30 pm	Popeye Film Festival (Chester Square)

Saturday, September 11, 1999

8:30 am	Popeye's 5K Run/Walk & 1.5 Mile Fun Run/Walk/Skate (BV Bank Parking Lot)
9:00 am - 9:00 pm	Popeye Museum (Spinach Can Collectibles)
9:00 am - 2:00 pm	Volksmarch 5/10K Walk (Chester Pizza Hut)
10:00 am - 5:00 pm	Olive Oyl's Cafe/Arts & Crafts (St. John's Parish Hall)
10:30 am - 7:00 pm	McMurtry's Petting Zoo (Picnic Area)
11:30 am	Popeye's Parade (High School to Courthouse)
12:00 pm	Carnival & Stands Open (Picnic Grounds)
2:00 pm - 3:00 pm	Lawrence Gregory - Illusionist (VFW Hall)
2:00 pm - 5:00 pm	Band - "Ned Grey & Friends" (Across from K of C Hall)
2:00 pm - 5:00 pm	Harvey the Juggler (Picnic Area)
5:30 pm - 8:30 pm	Washer Tournament (Check-in 5 pm) (Across from K of C Hall)
6:00 pm	Swee' Pea Race (St. Mary's School Area)
7:00 pm - 8:00 pm	Lawrence Gregory - Illusionist (VFW Hall)
7:15 pm - 7:45 pm	Classic Country Kickers (VFW Lot)
8:00 pm - 11:00 pm	Teen Dance - DJ (Picnic Area)
8:00 pm	Dance - "Night Shift" (VFW Parking Lot)
9:00 pm - 10:00 pm	Lawrence Gregory - Illusionist (VFW Hall)
9:30 pm	Popeye Film Festival (Chester Square)

Sunday, September 12, 1999

8:00 am - 4:00 pm	Popeye's Car Show (Chester High School)
9:00 am	Top of the Hill Volleyball (Cole Memorial Park)
10:00 am - 4:00 pm	Olive Oyl's Cafe/Arts & Crafts (St. John's Parish Hall)
11:00 am - 2:00 pm	Smorgasbord (K of C Hall)
11:30 am - 12:30 pm	Lawrence Gregory - Illusionist (VFW Hall)
12:00 pm	Carnival & Stands Open (Picnic Grounds)
12:00 pm - 1:30 pm	Lawn Mower Races (Check-in at 11:00 am) (Chester High School Area)
12:00 pm - 6:00 pm	McMurtry's Petting Zoo (Picnic Area)
1:00 pm - 4:00 pm	Model RC Plane Show (Cohen Complex Breezy Hill)
1:00 pm - 4:00 pm	Harvey the Juggler (Picnic Area)
1:00 pm - 4:00 pm	Band - "Ned Grey & Friends" (Across from K of C Hall)
1:00 pm - 5:00 pm	Special Bracelet Rides (Carnival)
2:00 pm	Sacred Concert (St. Mary's Church)
3:00 pm - 4:00 pm	Lawrence Gregory - Illusionist (VFW Hall)
4:30 pm	Amateur Hour Hidden Talent Show (VFW Parking Lot)
6:30 pm	Muny Band Concert (Picnic Grounds)
7:30 pm - 8:30 pm	Lawrence Gregory - Illusionist (VFW Hall)
9:15 pm	Fireworks
9:30 pm	Cash Giveaway Drawing (Central Stand)

In Case of Rain, Events Will be Held in St. Mary's Gym.

YANNI YANNI YANNI!!
YENNY YANNEE
YAN-EE YANNI
♡🏗👁◉📻 YANNI
YANNII!
YAHOOO
YANNIAIEI YANNIEIAO
Y A A A N N N I I I
YANNI
YANNII YANEE
YANNIMYMAN YANNI
YANNI

I L♥VE YANNII!!!!!

Ted L. Nancy, Director
560 No. Moorpark Rd. #236
Thousand Oaks, CA 91360   USA

DOKUZ EYLUL UNIVERSITY FACULTY OF FINE ARTS
Theater Arts Dept.

Izmir Turkey   ←———— Burger Spill   11/30/97

Dear Turkish Theater Dept.,

I want to put on the play "Annie" using a Turkish acting troupe.
I am seeking 71 Turkish performers, one with curly red hair. I
was referred to your fine department. Naturally, I expect to pay
to put on·this production. Let us talk about money for your
department. Who do I speak with?

Please send reply to Ted L. Nancy at The Turkish Annie Show 560
No. Moorpark Rd. #236. Thousand Oaks, CA 91360 USA. Please make
sure you refer to the "Turkish Annie Show" as I am also mounting a
Bulgarian production of "Oklahoma."

I have admired Turkish performances before. The acting is very
intense. Plus the cigarettes add smoke that is needed to create
atmosphere.

Thank you. I look forward to a mutually satisfying rendition of
this fun play of a balding old man and a dog.

Sincerely,

Ted L. Nancy

Ted L. Nancy

DOKUZ EYLÜL UNIVERSITY
FACULTY OF FINE ARTS
THEATRE ARTS DEPARTMENT

Mr. Ted L. Nancy, Director
560 No. Moorpark Rd. # 236
Thousand Oaks, CA 91360
USA

İzmir, Dec. 30, 1997

Dear Mr. Nancy,

   I have received your letter only yesterday, which means mailing letters are not any more sufficient enough to communicate. I would prefer fax or e-mail for a rapid response. If you have a fax, please, send to me the number.

   I am the ▓▓▓ of the Theatre Department in İzmir, and also a professional theatre director, active in every part of Turkey and abroad. I must confess that when I got your letter, I thought one of my friends in the USA is making fun of me. A Turkish *Annie Get Your Gun* with Turkish actors would be very interesting, indeed. Would you kindly give me some information about yourself and more about the project of Turkish *Annie* ? Are you considering it to produce in the States? Or in Turkey? If it will be in the States, then all the air fares, wages, etc. would rather be expensive. A second problem is the time and the duration of the rehearsals and the performances. You demand 71 Turkish performers, which is very hard to find that number of actors at the moment, since we're in the middle of the theatre season, as it is so elsewhere. But as soon as I get the necessary information from you, I can handle the matter quite smoothly.

   You sound to know the Turkish acting. Have you been in Turkey? Or did you see some of the actors while visiting USA? As you see I have many question marks in my mind. Will you please clear them up for me for the sake of this project! Let us correpond through telefax, which will speed the things up. I am going to give you a complete itinary for corresponding:

Banana

   I look forward to a detailed letter about yourself and your project and best wishes for the New Year!

← Coffee Mug

560 N Moorpark Rd. #236
Thousand Oaks, CA 91360 USA

Oct 8, 1998

PROF. DR.  ← relish

Izmir, Turkey

Dear Prof.  ← Ketchup JAM
I am sorry it took so long to write back. I have been zebra
teasing in New Zealand and was bitten.

Now with regards to the "Turkish Annie Show": I have had to
abandon that idea because of the 25 million dollar budget. I was
short in raising the money. Lots of people bailed out. I can do
a cheaper Turkish Annie with 7 sets of twins and a mirror. But
will it look as good? Will the quality still be there?

However, I am now putting my energies into a semi glitzy
"Turkish Pippin."

This will be Turkey's grandest production. The Titanic of
Pippins. Everyone will come.

The same actor that did "Bernard Blows His Cheek Out" the French
Cap d'or film winner will play the lead. He is committed. Can I
count on you as director? How do I reach you? What is the best
way to address this with you?

I will now only use 5 twins and a mirror but the quality will lend
itself to this most fantastic Pippin. Will you take the helm?
When will you arrive? Where can we talk?

I look forward to a reply from you.

Sincerely,

Ted L. Nancy

Prof. Dr.

the Art Committee,
State Theatres
Turkey

Mr. Ted L. Nancy, Director
560 No. Moorpark Rd. # 236
Thousand Oaks, CA 91360
USA

İzmir, October 19, 1998

Dear Mr. Nancy,

One busy year passed away since your letter of October 11, 1997, and my reply to you on December 30, 1997. I received your second letter dated October 8, 1998. only yesterday, and responding you right away. Yet I still float in a sea of doubts; you haven't answered my questions that I put forth in my previous letter. As you may well know that I am a professional in my field and care for a concrete perspective of your project. I would like to repeat my question once again with hope and appreciation:

1. Would you kindly give me more details about yourself?
2. I would very much appreciate if you could give me a more detailed description of your new project, ""Turkish Pippin".
3. Are you considering it to produce it in the States, or in Turkey?
4. You sound to know the Turkish acting: have you been in Turkey, or did you see some of the Turkish actors visiting USA.
5. Do you still need Turkish actors and actresses?

You ask if you could count me as director. Yes, of course; but if the production will be in the States, I have to make my schedule, and clear up all my activities in Turkey, where at the moment I am directing two plays in my private theatre, giving actor training courses, and acting as adviser to master and doctor students at the university, plus I am working on a book called *The* ⬛rary ← ?
What will be your offering for my work. You have to pay for my two-way air fares, and my residence in the States. When all these are defined with certitude I 'will take the helm'.

I look forward to a reply from you.

Best regards.

 ← Coffee again

560 No. Moorpark Rd. #236
Thousand Oaks, CA 91360   USA

PROF. DR.
Dokuz Eylul University
Theater Arts Dept.

Ismir, Turkey   May 18, 1999

Dear Prof. Dr.   ← OiNTMeNT

I am sorry I have not written sooner but I was Rhinoceros smirking
in New Guinea and was trampled. My torso was swollen up like a
balloon.

Now down to business: With regards to the Turkish "Oklahoma" that
I want to produce. (The Turkish "Pippen" is no more.)

I will need 2 Curley's. One at 360 pounds and one at 108 pounds
after dysentery hits him. This is the wasted away Curley. We go
from "Oh What A Beautiful Morning" to "Oh What A Case of The Runny
Trots." The whole 2nd act bridges on this. The actor who was in
"Bernard Blows His Cheek Out" was run over by a bus. He is out of
the production. Instead, I MAY have an adult film star that looks
like Roy Clark. He was last in "Hot Turkey Sandwich" the sassy
risque adult film.

Can we mount the play in Izmir in a 60,000 seat arena? Can I do
it with 3 actors and a pulley system and 2 shards of mirror?
We will give out sunshine plops at the door to the first 59,000
people. Or we can give out spongy sniffs. It's up to you.

Will you take the helm? Can you steer the ship? Lets talk
turkey! Tell me about odor from bladder leakage. What do we do
about that? I look forward to hearing from you soon. Will you
stretch my gum?

Now about me: You asked for my resume. I have an extensive
resume which I have included for your perusal.

Sincerely,

Ted L. Nancy

RESUME

TED L. NANCY

560 No. Moorpark Rd.
Apt #236
Thousand Oaks, CA 91360

1996-1997   Clam World   CLAMS MANAGER
                                       Contact: Doyle Fludge

Backword

Jerry Seinfeld
New York City
(address withheld)

Ted Nancy
560 No. Moorpark #236
Thousand Oaks, CA 91360

Dear Mr. Nancy,

My name is Jerry Seinfeld. I am the co-creator and star of the most successful network television sitcom of all time. (I got some help with the writing and acting.) But I feel now the time is right for a new project with a new feeling and here it is.

I would like to move my entire apartment building from Central Park West in New York City to No. Moorpark Road in Thousand Oaks very near you. I am hoping to "make this happen" on or around Memorial Day. This is going to be a very costly operation, but I am an international star on a national holiday and I have so much money it would choke a horse. (Which I have done. It takes roughly $6,000 in twenties. You could also do it with singles, but I like to be a sport.)

Here's my problem, which I would like to make yours. I would like to do this while the current residents are still in the building and without their knowledge. I have heard that when it comes to deceiving innocent, unassuming, everyday people with a load of unadulterated B.S., you are the best out there. So you think you could keep Beverly Sills distracted while I moved this exclusive, upscale doorman building 3,000 miles to California? What about Phyllis Newman and Adolph Green? Remember, these people know Broadway and have heard every trick in the book. We don't want another *Towering Inferno* scene here. Do you think you could put it over on them? Come on, let's get me living out on No. Moorpark in the lifestyle to which I have grown accustomed!

Remember, I am a hugely famous and fabulously wealthy star and have not heard the word "no" since the late '80s. Also, I will need some burly, intimidating doormen who can send people back to their apartments if anyone tries to get out during the 17 weeks it will take to uproot the structure, transport it, and then refasten it to No. Moorpark. (I have had a teleconference with Vince McMahon. I couldn't believe his prices for a couple of goons on Memorial Day. I mean really "out of whack.") Perhaps you know someone who is more in whack. Also, I'll need provisions for a large number of rats, cockroaches and pigeons that are coming with me (separate container).

Mr. Nancy, I have every confidence that Thousand Oaks can absorb the wealthy, pampered, somewhat demanding workforce the residents of the building can provide. (I am still working out how to pipeline the necessary smoked salmon and whitefish it takes to keep this place running.) Also, it would help during the re-orientation phase if the shop owners on No. Moorpark could rig their doors so it's necessary to press a small white button before entering.

I am proud to say no one in Central Park West history has ever undertaken a project of this scope. This constitutes a great coming together of something; of which a part I hope you will be of.

Thank you again for your consideration. Remember, Mr. Nancy, this is not a prank. We must not displease El Presidente. Here's to wishing us luck. If this all goes well, there should be no apartments available in the building when we arrive.

I have to go now; more residuals and fine cigars are coming in. Is it hard to get brass grommets out there? I am going to need roughly a million of them (goldish color) to make sure there's no further tampering after the re-dedication.

Wishing you a life of elegant elegance like I have,

Jerry Seinfeld